How to survive the
CREDIT CRUNCH

"Neither a borrower
nor a lender be,
For loan oft loses both
itself and friend."

PLAYWRIGHT WILLIAM SHAKESPEARE

IN HAMLET ACT 1 SCENE 3

CIRCA 1602

"Can I borrow $700bn, please?"

UNITED STATES TREASURY SECRETARY
HENRY 'HANK' PAULSON TO CONGRESS

IN DEEP TROUBLE

SEPTEMBER 2008

How to survive the
CREDIT
CRUNCH

101 TOP TIPS ON HOW TO *BEAT* THE CREDIT CRISIS!

PUBLISHER Damien Moore

ART DIRECTOR Amanda Lunn

PROJECT EDITOR Jennifer Close

PROJECT ART EDITOR Sharon Cluett

First published in the United Kingdom
in 2008 by

studio cactus

13 SOUTHGATE STREET WINCHESTER
HAMPSHIRE SO23 9DZ
TEL 01962 878600
MAIL@STUDIOCACTUS.CO.UK
WWW.STUDIOCACTUS.CO.UK

Conceived and produced by Studio
Cactus Ltd

Text copyright © 2008 Associated
Newspapers

A CIP catalogue record for this book is
available from the British Library

ISBN: 978-1-904239-09-3

Printed and bound in Great Britain by
Short Run Press

CONTENTS

Foreword

This is Money is a proud institution. A decade after it was conceived it is now arguably the country's most trusted source of online independent financial news, information and advice.

We aim to deliver to our 1.6 million monthly readers the most important financial information to help them make the right decisions about their money. The editorial team, which is entirely independent of commercial bias, has a reputation for accuracy, plain English and for breaking big news stories.

Since the credit crunch hit, we have been providing up-to-the-minute news and analysis that explains not only what is happening as it happens but also how to shelter against the fallout from the global lending squeeze.

Our safe savings section provided unsurpassed coverage of how to protect hard-earned money from the black hole caused by a growing number of banking failures.

The in-depth coverage is backed up with tips, tools, guides, calculators and advice to help save money and make money in all aspects of life.

We also work hard to stop punters getting ripped off and have a strong reputation for fighting the corner for wronged individuals, winning dozens of victories against many of the big names in the financial world.

We have been relentlessly naming and shaming shoddy financial services firms, including leading banks and building societies, since 1999, while the campaigning reputation and editorial independence of our parent group, Associated Newspapers, dates back more than a century.

On top of all this, we now have this fantastic book to add to our armoury.

Author Richard Browning has written a light-hearted but deadly serious guide to show how small adjustments in our attitudes to money can reap huge rewards and help ward off any spectres the credit crunch may throw at us.

For an in-depth economic analysis of the credit crunch, I suggest you take a look at books written by my colleagues on the *Daily Mail* and *Mail on Sunday* respectively. They are, *The Crunch: How Greed and Incompetence Sparked the Credit Crisis* by Alex Brummer and *The Gods That Failed: How the Financial Elite Have Gambled Away Our Futures* by Larry Elliott and Dan Atkinson.

Ours is written for the man and woman on the street. I hope you find it as useful and entertaining as I did.

ANDREW OXLADE
Editor, *This is Money*, and financial pundit for ITV's *This Morning*

Crunch time

The United Kingdom is in trouble.

Collectively we owe £1.4 trillion – £1,400,000,000,000 – across credit cards, loans and mortgages. That's more than the value of the economy itself; more than the total worth of the country's financial output in terms of the money we spend, the money the Government spends, the money we invest and our net exports.

For someone to earn that kind of money on an average salary of £26,000 would take more than 53 million years. Add another 13 million years if you want it net of tax and National Insurance. These are big numbers. And it's payback time.

This may all sound rather glib but debts at these levels can only be sustained when the economy is growing. And those days are over. Households have seen their expenditures rocket as energy and food prices have soared. Banks are charging ever higher rates on personal loans and mortgages. And unemployment is due to reach levels not seen since Margaret Thatcher was Prime Minister. Even if we wanted to, we can't borrow our way out because the banks have stopped lending to each other – a phenomenon known as a credit crunch – and they've stopped lending to us. How we got into this mess will be dealt with later but first, let's take a look at the crunch itself.

In the summer of 2007, the *This is Money* team were poring over the crop of business magazines when one of the American economics titles fell open at a picture that was trying to tell a story. A big story. In the drawing, arrows pointed out from little pictures of houses to pictures of banks. More arrows joined more banks and another arrow pointed across the sea to the rest of the world. There was a final big arrow that pointed downwards.

The implications seemed incomprehensible. The suggestion was that houses in America were somehow going to take down the US banking system and the rest of the world with it. The article was lacking on detail but it did mention collateralized debt obligations, or CDOs.

Now, we'd heard of them. We'd received emails from readers in the USA asking why a website of our status hadn't written about CDOs. They were, it was claimed by the correspondents, the safest and most lucrative type of investment there had ever been.

The big rating agencies – statistics experts who mark investments out of 10 depending on how risky they are – gave them AAA status. Top marks. Whatever they were, these things were safe and promised returns of up to 10%.

But as a rule of thumb, when the man and woman in the street starts talking about sure-fire investment opportunities, the time to invest is over – and it's time to start smelling a rat. And this rat stank.

CDOs, along with other equally complicated and unregulated investment vehicles, consisted of packaged-up mortgage debt, sold as investments by bankers and other faceless financial "experts" to other bankers and financial institutions. When you bought in, any returns would be based on the ongoing mortgage repayments from the homeowners.

These types of investment were concocted in the late 1980s and had relatively short track records, but it is on past performance that the ratings agencies base their "intelligence". Data for mortgage repayments for the past decade looked good. House prices had been rising, the sizes of mortgages were rising and mortgage repayments were rising. They were a safe bet.

Unfortunately, they overlooked two vital elements.
1. House prices can fall.
2. People on low incomes often can't afford to keep up their mortgage payments.

For years up until 2007, there had been a feeling in some quarters of the USA and the UK that house prices would keep rising for ever. And while banks were prepared to lend whatever it took and estate agents were prepared to push asking prices to whatever they could, house prices did keep rising. But unless wages rise in line with house prices, growth in the housing market becomes unsustainable. In 2007, it began to unravel.

In America, lenders and brokers had been arranging mortgages for people on extremely low incomes – people who never had a chance of paying the money back. There was a slight possibility that if house prices *could* rise for ever, that if these people defaulted they would be able to sell their homes for a profit. But that's not what happened. These loans were called "subprime" – a fancy word for "not very good". The mortgage salesmen were offering nominal interest rates for the first few months. Long enough for them to take their commission and disappear. Long enough for the loans to be carved up and sold on as part of a complex investment package and long enough before the world realised that, in fact, these loans were toxic.

By the autumn of 2007 it was clear that subprime homeowners had been sold up the river. House prices were plummeting and they were being evicted in their thousands. It was also becoming clear that the investments based on these people's ability to repay their mortgages were worthless. The trouble was, these investments were so complex and spread out among the world's banks and finance houses that no one knew how much was at stake or which banks were at risk if it went wrong. We still don't.

"Simplicity is the ultimate sophistication."

LEONARDO DA VINCI. ARTIST, INVENTOR,
MATHEMATICIAN, YOU NAME IT...

What we do know is that seemingly overnight banks stopped lending. The world credit markets seized up and created what we know as the credit crunch. They didn't trust each other. They probably didn't even trust themselves.

Northern Rock was the first British bank to fall as a result of the credit crunch. In February 2008, after an emergency loan from the Bank of England caused panic among savers and sparked the first "run" on a British bank since the 1860s, it was nationalised. The Government had little choice. The alternative would have been a high-profile, High Street humiliation for the bank, the customers, the economy, the Government and the country.

Northern Rock had been one of the most aggressive lenders. In the months running up to its demise it was throwing money at homeowners at such a rate that one in five new mortgages were on its books. But rather than using income from savers to balance the books it was financing its loans with money borrowed from the money markets – other banks and financial institutions.

Its behaviour seemed to mirror that of the British people.

A NATION IN DEBT

During his 10-year reign as Chancellor, the now Prime Minister Gordon Brown often boasted of a proud record of economic stability: steady economic growth, stable exchange rates, low interest rates and low unemployment. And an inflation rate that remained at 3% or less for 16 years – a phenomenon not seen since 1945.

It is a record that anyone at the helm could be proud of. Unfortunately, economic growth requires each of the components of the economy to grow. In other words, spending. And spend we did.

Now, there's nothing wrong with spending. Without it the economy shrinks, companies lay off staff and eventually go out of business. If the rot is not halted it can spiral to a messy conclusion. There is also nothing wrong with borrowing. Anyone who starts a business will usually prepare a business plan and present it to a bank or an investor with a view to borrowing money to get the project off the ground. The credit crunch has shown what can happen if the sources of credit dry up.

The trouble was, fuelled by years of historically low interest rates, we borrowed far, far too much. And now it's turning nasty.

HOW WE GOT INTO THIS MESS

A lot of commentators use economic models, historic similes and fancy jargon to explain what went wrong. And a lot of people find that kind of analysis comforting. I don't. I want to tell you a story, a potted history of *This is Money* if you like…

In the first few months of the new millennium I was working on the planning stages of a major publishing project and we were looking for themes that summed up the state of the nation. News, fashion, sport, celebrity, the usual suspects were all there – but there was something missing. We needed to tap further into the zeitgeist than B-list celebrities and football. Checking the mailbag it became obvious. People were starting to seriously worry about their debts. Brilliant. We'd launch with a big get-out-of-debt campaign. That was in early 2000.

Now, for various reasons the project was shelved – along with our debt campaign. But that didn't matter any longer because within a year the mood of the country had changed. The Bank Rate (formerly the Base Rate) remained steady in 2000 but by early 2001 it began its steady decline. Money was becoming cheaper and cheaper. Previously rational people were quickly drawn into a crazy borrowing binge, egged on by brokers, banks and other lenders who began goading people into taking on more and more credit.

Suddenly, it felt like everyone had gone out and bought a new car or two. People were having fancy new kitchens and Roman-style bathrooms installed like they were going out of fashion, which, incidentally, they now are. Builders were adding extra rooms to homes, where previously they would have been deemed illegal. It became impossible to get a plumber to visit unless you were looking to install an entire new central-heating system.

But pay wasn't rising much above inflation. And inflation was low. So where was the money coming from? Why, from house prices, of course.

By now I was working for *This is Money* in the development hub in "new-media land". It was exciting and we were creating things that had never been done before with a talented young team, staffed by college leavers and other, well, let's call them first-time buyers. Being the only person from the money team in that building, conversations often turned to money-related issues. It was great to see people taking an interest in such matters. But increasingly the conversations were not about the stock market, interest rates and Isas but about debt. Not about how to get out of it, but how to get more.

The country's collective attitude to debt had completely changed. Never mind that it could take a lifetime to clear a £30,000 credit card debt and that anyone with common sense should try to live within their means, that was irrelevant for people leaving university with up to £15,000 debts to show for their education.

Over the next couple of years, some of these youngsters had not only bought their first flat but within six months of doing it had remortgaged to buy stuff and go on holiday on the back of the rise in its value.

It wasn't just youngsters, of course; everyone seemed to be playing the remortgaging game. And word was out about another game, in which you could beat the credit card companies by maxing out the debt available on a string of 0% interest deals that were suddenly all the rage. "Free money" was there for the taking.

But what happened next would affect the youngsters most and by 2003 they were in a fix.

The credit boom was over. House prices had peaked. The cost of a one-bedroom flat was now out of reach of the average first-time buyer on the income multiples that sensible lenders were prepared to offer. It was time to settle down and wait for wage inflation to close the gap and breathe life back into the market.

But it didn't happen that way. Word soon spread that loans were being offered based, not on income, but on perceived affordability. It didn't take long for everyone trying to break into the housing market to contact a mortgage broker to try to get hold of bigger and bigger loans.

By now even the local newsagent was advising his customers on how they could get into the housing market as a first-time buyer and as a buy-to-let investor – a sure sign that the boom time was over. But it wasn't. Estate agents were pricing homes on a see-what-we-can-get-away-with basis. And with lenders willing to lend just about anything to just about anyone – even the unemployed and people prepared to lie about their incomes – the boom continued for another four years.

And so here we are now, and the game's over. No one knows the extent of the damage we're about to face. How far house prices will fall as a result of years of recklessness is anyone's guess. If the jobless figures continue to rise and mortgage lenders, banks and credit-card companies start calling in the debts the scenario almost doesn't bear thinking about.

Mercifully, inflation looks like it will fall as the price of oil continues to settle at an affordable level. And as a result we can expect interest rates to remain steady and even fall throughout 2009. One thing is for sure. We are heading for recession. But how bad could it really get?

THE GREAT ESCAPE?

At the time of publication, there is some evidence that the credit crunch is easing – very slightly. Following the collapse of high-profile banks in the USA and Iceland, huge cash injections into the banking system from governments on either side of the Atlantic appear to be restoring confidence and trust between the world's banks.

Gordon Brown instigated a £50 billion nationalisation of major British banks. So far the Government has bought stakes in Royal Bank of Scotland, HBOS and Lloyds TSB. Unfortunately, banks don't appear to trust one another enough yet to lower the intra-bank interest rates – Libor – at which they lend to each other. Until that happens the public is unlikely to see any benefit – even if the Bank of England cuts the official Bank Rate.

The government bailouts began in the USA when the Treasury Secretary Henry "Hank" Paulson called on fellow American politicians to back a $700 billion cash injection into the financial system aimed at drawing a line under the toxic-loans debacle. But they said "no".

In time-honoured fashion when things don't go your way first time, he asked again. There was still much dissent. The politicians represented constituents who were suffering from rising unemployment, record petrol prices and falling house prices and who were asking why they should bail out overpaid, incompetent bankers who had created the mess they were in.

But the alternative was much worse.

HOW COULD IT END? THE WORST CASE SCENARIO

If the banking system was allowed to collapse there would be no more money available. If banks closed down, people wouldn't receive their salaries. Without money to borrow, businesses that relied on debt to finance their operations would close. As people lost their jobs, there would be spin-off closures in shops and any number of services and related businesses.

Quickly, the economy would seize up completely, leading in all probability to civil disobedience, food riots and ultimately war. Hungry people will do whatever it takes.

Soon, whether or not to have children becomes a purely financial decision. If couples only have one child, there are no more brothers and sisters, aunts, uncles and cousins and the population halves. If they choose not to have children at all, the population dies out within a generation. No money. No people. The end.

Thankfully it's not that bad. You can come back out from behind the sofa. Human beings are far more resilient than letting a few irresponsible bankers bring an end to civilisation. And besides, the US taxpayer had just pumped $700 billion into the system. That would help. Everybody said so.

Well, not exactly. In fact, not at all. Once the bailout had been agreed, the value of shares across the globe went into freefall. And in a market where the value of companies is measured by the number of shares in circulation and the price of those shares, when the price hits a low-enough point, the company becomes worthless.

Former financial behemoth Lehman Brothers had already gone bust and others such as Bear Stearns had to be rescued. Rescues were taking place all over the world, including in the recently booming economy of Iceland where the government is nationalising its biggest banks. The eventual outcome of this mess remains uncertain. There are still unanswered questions and more revelations are likely to come out in the wash. There's a particularly dark shadow hanging over the insurance sector because of the liabilities they may face, having underwritten some of the toxic debts. If there is any fallout, and it spreads across the industry it could have far reaching implications. As with all of this, no one knows.

HOW DOES ALL THIS AFFECT YOU AND ME?

We already know that mortgage lenders are charging a lot more than they were before the credit crunch. Hundreds of loans have been withdrawn from the market and those that are available come with higher interest rates and massive arrangement fees (or interest in advance, as it is known).

Lenders are slashing the percentage of a home's value that they're prepared to lend on. Any recovery led by first-time buyers seems a long way off if deposits of 25% become the norm. The days of 100% mortgages are well and truly over and people coming off attractive fixed-rate deals are likely to be paying a lot more than they had bargained for. That's if they can remortgage at all.

Personal loans are already dearer and harder to come by and, to a lesser extent, the irresponsibility of credit card companies, which has yet to come to the fore, is likely to result in fewer deals available and fewer successful applications. Such a move will hurt anyone who has been lured on to 0% cards and who doesn't have the means to clear the debt once the interest-free period expires.

Thankfully, the price of oil, which had reached unprecedented highs and was a contributing factor in the massive rises in food prices,

started to subside as demand fell in the shrinking global economy.
This is good news all round. That means prices of food, transport and
domestic fuel should at least stabilise.

But we cannot be complacent. The banks may have been bailed out
but they still want their money back and the days of living on the
never-never are over. And this is where the fun starts. Forget that you
may have no choice, it can be fun to be frugal. There are all kinds of
knock-on benefits you can enjoy if you tweak the way you live and
change your attitude to how you spend what money's left in the kitty.
For one, you may learn – or remember – how to enjoy yourself without
spending huge sums of money. I know, I already live like that. I had my
fingers burned in the years leading up to recession in the early 90s and
have been passing on my survival techniques to readers of *This is
Money* in the form of simple, and yes fun, saving tips.

And if there appears to be no silver lining to the current economic
cloud then there is at least a green one. There are noticably fewer cars
on the road for one thing and if no amount of coaxing and cajoling by
the greens has made us slow down on the roads and follow the
laudable mantra "reduce, reuse, recycle", it's clear that the assault on
our wallets is proving to be a much more powerful incentive. Many of
my saving tips are good for the planet as well as my pocket, which is
why I'm being called the "accidental environmentalist".

The tips in the book cover all kinds of situations and dilemmas we'll
need to face up to as we try to make ends meet in the battle to reduce
our debts. They'll take you from the kitchen, through the garage via
the loft and into the garden, along the motorway, to the shops and
even abroad. There's a world of money-saving potential out there.

But first let's take a look at some of the wider issues.

AT HOME

TEN OF THE BEST

- Cut the cost of your fuel bills *(see p.38)*
- Consider installing a water meter *(see p.39)*
- Cut your home phone bills *(see p.40)*
- Sell your clutter – or give it away *(see p.48)*
- Do DIY – but do it properly, please *(see p.51)*
- Shop around for cheaper home insurance *(see p.52)*
- Do you need all those TV channels? *(see p.85)*
- Shop online *(see p.89)*
- How to choose a builder *(see p.106)*
- Make do and mend *(see p.107)*

The place to start looking for ways to change your lifestyle and your costly habits is under your nose – at home. You barely need to lift a finger to start making big savings.

If you have a computer, fire it up and run through the *Ten of the best* (*see opposite*) to see whether you can cut the cost of those unavoidable expenses such as fuel, water, insurance and phone bills. Ask yourself, too, when you last watched all the extra subscription channels you're paying a small fortune for.

If you're still at the computer think about ordering your shopping online. It's a fabulous way of cutting out the impulse purchases and cutting down the wear and tear on your car – and the petrol bill. It's been out of the news lately, but the looming environmental crisis shows no sign of abating. Using the car less is one step towards becoming an accidental environmentalist. If we don't make an effort now, it's not hard to imagine a time when the freedom to use our car is curtailed by the courts.

And when was the last time you bothered to take a look through the boxes in the loft? You may not have a treasure trove but as far as someone else is concerned it could be just what they're looking for. Selling the unwanted clutter from home may be an easy target for the satirists but it's also an easy way to make some cash to help make ends meet.

If you're doggedly anti-DIY but have mounting bills and unavoidable repairs, now may be the time to get some quality training from the adult education college. The small cost of the course should soon pay dividends.

ON FOOD

TEN OF THE BEST

Did you know we chuck one third of the food we buy in the bin? This is a Government statistic. It's slightly misleading because it includes leftovers and food items we cannot eat such as teabags. But it's all part of the ongoing shock tactics designed to turn us into a waste-free nation of recyclers and healthy eaters. If we managed what we bought properly there wouldn't be any leftovers.

But the really shocking Government statistic concerns the food that we buy to eat and then throw out because we don't get around to eating it. And that amounts to £600 a year for a family and £420 for an individual. The fact that we throw any food away is scandalous. The fact that it amounts to so much financial waste means if we can tackle it tomorrow, we've already got a few hundred quid in the bank with the smallest amount of effort.

There's an initial hurdle to overcome when changing our habits. And it takes a little thought and small amount of planning. But once we start this journey – buying only what we can and want to eat – a whole new world of healthy eating awaits.

One small change to our behaviour that not only saves money but could also have massively beneficial knock-on effects is to start using the local market. It should be the lifeblood of the community.

If we all started to use our markets there would be more than an evens chance that our town centres might survive the relentless expansion of the big supermarkets. If more people came back into our towns, we could see a resurgence of quality butchers, bakers and people who make things.

It's surely worth a try. The weekly shopping bill is the big one and if you're lucky enough to have access to a market more than once a week, you can really make a dent in any overspending.

ON MONEY

£

TEN OF THE BEST

- Change your attitude to your mortgage (*see p.36*)
- Clear your credit card debt (*see p.37*)
- Claim your benefits and tax credits (*see p.83*)
- Avoid the payment protection racket (*see p.87*)
- Reclaim your bank charges (*see p.99*)
- Credit card tarts may look sweet but... (*see p.101*)
- Earn more money (*see p.119*)
- Do you know how much you spend? (*see p.128*)
- Avoid loyalty cards at all costs (*see p.132*)
- Avoid cashback credit cards (*see p.133*)

The best way to cut back is to spend less. The best way to destroy the economy is to spend nothing at all.

Managing your money is all about finding the right balance between healthy spending and enjoyment. If we can take a look at some of the causes of the big-ticket money worries and change the way we think about those we'll soon be on the way to happier, wealthier times.

It's amazing how many of us don't even know where the money goes, and how many of us refuse to claim benefits as a matter of principle. How many of us stick with the same bank because we've always stuck with the same bank? And how many of us have been sold a stinker of an insurance policy that we're not even aware of?

An alternative to spending less is earning more. For many people, however, the idea of a second job is bordering on the abhorrent. If you've already done a week's work the last thing on your mind, after sleep, is going back to work again. But, as is the case with many of the tips in this book, it comes down to whether or not you are able to change your attitude. Has it ever crossed your mind that another job might be fun? And need only be temporary? Around Christmas and Easter there's likely to be more interesting choices and let's not forget that change, they say, is as good as a cliche about having a rest. It is certainly better, in my world, than staying in and watching an episode of *EastEnders* or *Pro-Celebrity Wife Swap in the Jungle*.

In fact, I still have fond memories of being up to my neck in grease undoing rusted scaffolding joints and of working in a cinema, watching the same film more than 60 times. Even stuffing envelopes – with a great bunch of people – was a satisfying experience. It could be a doubly valuable way to use a week or two of your holiday entitlement if, rather than jetting off to an expensive resort for your fill of sangria and sardines, you fill your ailing coffers with cash.

ON LIFESTYLE

TEN OF THE BEST

- Use your talent to earn extra cash (*see p.50*)

- Learn to say "no" (*see p.61*)

- The cost of keeping up appearances (*see p.64*)

- Cut down your drinking (*see p.72*)

- Meet your new friends: Citizens Advice (*see p.90*)

- Take up a money-saving hobby (*see p.93*)

- When it comes to fashion, sizes matters (*see p.108*)

- Learn to use a computer – and to type (*see p.112*)

- Make the most of your lunch break (*see p.122*)

- It's good to talk – no, it's vital (*see p.145*)

If your life is a rollercoaster of exotic weekends away, meals out, heavy drinking sessions, a flash car, the finest clothes, the best phone, binge shopping, cupboards full of things you've forgotten you had – a permanent high as you rush between work and play without a care in the world...

Why?

There's more to life than you. And there's more to you than what you own and a full diary.

If such a high-octane lifestyle has left you with a correspondingly high credit card debt, now's the time to seek out the simpler things in life. It's much more rewarding than shouting into a mobile phone because you're running late.

It's not just the i-generation: iPods, iPhones, i, i, i, me, me, me; we've all been guilty of overindulgence to a lesser or greater extent, carried away on the meteoric rise of the housing market ... but meteors don't rise, they fall.

If going out is your only interest, try staying in. Instead of going out and blowing £100 on a night out you don't remember, why not cultivate that creative side that you've been ignoring all these, years: dust off that violin, revisit that novel you started to write, strip down that old mountain bike that's rusting away in the garage. A revolution in your life is waiting for you to make it happen.

Take a look at some of these lifestyle tips. You could soon become a much more rounded (likeable) person with some genuine long-term friendships and money in your pocket.

ON THE ROAD

TEN OF THE BEST

Has anyone else noticed fewer cars on the roads since the beginning of the year? One factor will be that car sales have fallen off the proverbial cliff (down more than 20% in September 2008). But it also suggests that there are people with cars that they're no longer using – because they never needed them in the first place.

It's interesting to see how quickly a combination of higher petrol prices and the lending squeeze can start to clear streets within a few months. There are environmental benefits to free market forces, after all.

After your home, one of the most expensive items you're likely to buy is your car. Unless you live in deepest rural Britain the chances are you may not need it. Many families certainly don't need two.

The associated expenses can be random and debilitating. Has anyone else noticed an increasing number of newer cars on the roads with dents that haven't been repaired?

Assuming that needs must, there are ways of cutting down that you may not have thought about.

Did you know there are scores of alternatives to the breakdown cover offered by the AA and RAC? It may even come with your car insurance if you check the small print. And have you added up how much you spend over a year at those hand car washes?

Recent news of a proliferation in speed cameras that will track entire journeys should send shivers through every driver. Finding ways of avoiding speeding fines could soon be the major way of cutting the cost of motoring. Check out the *Ten of the best* to find out more.

ON GOING GREEN

TEN OF THE BEST

- Dump your car altogether (*see p.67*)
- Walk or cycle to the station/work (*see p.68*)
- Ask yourself: do I really need this? (*see p.70*)
- Grow your own herbs (*see p.104*)
- Neighbours: don't try to beat them, meet them (*see p.105*)
- Swap and share – books and more (*see p.118*)
- Drink tap water (*see p.120*)
- Cut down on the meat (*see p.124*)
- Turn down the heating (*see p.135*)
- Don't lose the plot – if you can get one, that is (*see p.148*)

On Going Green

The recycling lobby has a problem. Without a financial incentive many people simply aren't interested in diverting valuable time to sorting the cereal boxes from the drinks cartons and grading the types of paper that can be recycled and separating it from the envelopes, which cannot.

There is one kind of financial incentive – a backwards one – in the form of threats from local authorities, which impose fines on households who commit crimes such as placing twigs in with the general household waste. There's a long way to go before the public buys in to the recycling agenda.

For people living in flats, where there simply isn't the space for different bins for different types of waste, it's going to be difficult making the first steps en route to "planet green". And if you have to drive to the recycling facility, forget it.

But once you've caught the bug, you quickly become addicted. Landfill space is running out and you start to feel part of a sea change sweeping the country. Sooner or later we'll all have to play our part. But in the meantime, there are plenty of other ways you can flick the green switch while saving a stash of cash. Do you realise your car may be costing you £18,000 over three years without getting anywhere near to clearing the cost of buying it? Could you afford to get rid of it?

There was a time when people used to think nothing of walking 10 miles to work and back. Now we baulk at the idea of walking to the station. But you can walk a mile in just 20 minutes – a breeze if you've got your iPod blasting walk-faster music into your ears.

Even if you live in a flat, there's no excuse for not catching the grow-your-own bug. A windowsill is all that's needed for a summer-long herb garden. Gardening on any scale is a great way to meet the neighbours, which opens a whole world of exchange, whether it be tools, produce, or just interests.

101 WAYS TO SAVE MONEY

What follows are 101 ways to beat the credit crunch. Each tip is crafted to entertain as well as illustrate how we can all make big savings without much effort. The "Saving" figure at the bottom of each tip is a guide to the savings we may be able to make over a year if we put our minds to it.

Let's have some fun.

1

CAN YOU SEE
THE LIGHT?

If you have been reading the coverage of the ongoing credit crunch in the press and are now too terrified to open a newspaper or switch on the TV, this first tip is for you. It's a reminder that in spite of the news coverage of doom we need to keep a sense of perspective. The Worst Case Scenario (*see p.17*) is an unlikely hypothesis. The world isn'tt going to end just yet and thankfully we Brits possess enough of a sense of humour to survive anything that the global financial meltdown can throw at us. The credit crunch will be a whole lot easier to survive if we don't lose sight of that.

Frankly, given the combination of mind-bogglingly massive figures that mean less the more they appear and the behaviour of some of the world's apparently leading bankers that has been so stupefyingly cretinous and shocking, the only recourse sometimes is to try to see the funny side.

This book aims to marry the unlikely bedfellows of gloom and doom with humour and plenty of serious money-saving tips to help us get back on the straight and narrow.

Along with all the financial "things to think about", you'll find some of the tips in this book are such pure common sense that they are not too far removed from parody. And that's fine. A lot of people seemed to lose the traits of basic common sense over the past few years so I make no apology for that.

But I would suggest that for a true sense of how ridiculous the world became post-credit crunch you should – if you don't mind a bit of bad language – sign up for the newsletters from the two finest satirical online publications: The UK's *Daily Mash* and its American cousin, *The Onion*. They're free. And very funny. And don't forget to check my very own daily light-hearted money tip sheet, *This is Not Work*, as well as *This Is Money's* weekly round-up of all the financial news, tips and advice.

SAVING Your sanity.

2 Change your attitude to your mortgage

If you don't have your heart set on a bucket of De Beers diamonds or a Premiership football club, the most expensive item you are ever likely to buy is your home. And if you're not in the privileged position to pay cash, make sure the loan you use to finance it is the best available.

Until the credit crunch, the general rule was that a lender's standard variable rate (SVR) would cost you hundreds of pounds a year more than you needed to pay. But the crunch sent the rulebook flying out the window and almost daily it is being hastily rewritten – in the main to ensure that every new loan comes with a fee.

That said, there are enough deals around to make it worth a couple of hours of your life every year to check what's out there.

If you can afford to make overpayments on your mortgage you'll make massive savings. A £100,000 loan at 6% over 25 years costs £643 a month. Total interest: £93,000. But overpay by £100 a month and you'll be debt free six years early, saving a staggering £25,000 in interest.

SAVING £1,000s

www.thisismoney.co.uk/mortgage-finder
www.thisismoney.co.uk/mortgage-calculator
www.thisismoney.co.uk/mortgage-help

Clear your credit card debt

3

One of the golden rules of financial planning is to clear your most expensive debts first: in other words, your credit cards.

Ok, credit cards offer a convenient way to pay for goods and services but if you can't clear the balance every month, consider a low-cost loan as an alternative. Do the sums: a credit card debt (APR 16.8%) of say £2,500 over five years will cost £1,212 in interest. A loan at 7.8% will cost £527. A total saving of £685. Multiply that to £30,000 of debts on plastic and if you repay the minimum, which is likely to be around £430 a month, it will take nearly 23 years to clear the debt. Even just £5,000 at a mere £80 a month will take 12 years. What are your plans for the 2020s?

NOTE If you can clear the balance every month you should consider using your card for purchases over £100. A peculiar point of law – Section 75 of the Consumer Credit Act, to be precise – means the card company has to cough up if you buy something from a company that goes bust.

With recession looming, this is a particularly wise move if you are buying goods and services from companies that typically suffer in hard times, such as tickets from low-cost airlines or furniture that will only be delivered after several weeks in limbo.

SAVING £100s

www.thisismoney.co.uk/loans
www.thisismoney.co.uk/travel

4 Cut the cost of your fuel bills

As the global demand for power threatens to outstrip supply, prices are rising. But that doesn't mean you need to be ripped off.

Even though the suppliers seem to put their prices up more or less in unison, the domestic market for gas and electricity is, we're told, a competitive one. You can change supplier with a few clicks of the mouse and your new supplier will take care of the formalities – you just pay less every month.

If you're unsure about the calculations, or frankly can't quite believe them when you've run an online comparison, you can phone companies such as Simply Switch on 0800 954 00 30 and they'll talk you through it. Remember to arm yourself with a couple of recent bills before you call.

And if you are tempted to sign up to a capped tariff, remember this is a gamble where you're staking your piece of mind against the whims and greed of global oil and gas suppliers. Prices fluctuate (up and down) and you could end up stuck on a more expensive tariff only to watch prices fall.

SAVING £100s

www.thisismoney.co.uk/bills

Consider installing a water meter

5

We take our tap water for granted. And why not? The companies behind the supply exist to make a profit, we pay them for water and have every right to expect it to flow from our taps.

But if it doesn't rain, supply runs dry and the price goes up. So you may want to consider the possibility of installing a meter. If you have a big home with few occupants you'll perhaps be surprised to learn that you could halve your annual bill.

On the other side of the equation are the fears that once everyone has a meter installed the game's over. Once the money-saving benefits of a having a meter installed have been removed, they can start raising prices for everyone. That would mean you'd use less water – surely a good thing – but you might stop taking baths if you knew how much each one was costing.

Whether the environmental benefits outweigh the fact that these are private companies in business to make money (from you) for their shareholders is for you to decide. Do your homework.

SAVING £100s

www.ccwater.org.uk (Consumer Council for Water calculator)
www.thisismoney.co.uk/caring-consumer

6 Cut your home phone bills

BT may seem to behave like a monopoly but it most definitely is not one. If you must use your phone, there are scores of cheaper alternatives.

From the cable and TV companies that package up the phone, television and internet, the internet companies that give you free phone calls if you take their broadband, to the extreme low-cost dial-up services that give you access to cheaper calls using your existing BT line, the industry is awash with deals. Even the mobile phone companies are in on the landline and internet action. Beware. Phone companies are perpetually moving the goalposts and rewriting the small print and marketing blurb. Even with online call checkers, it is an excruciatingly time-consuming business trying to find the cheapest phone deals that work for you.

AUTHOR'S NOTE A BT phone line and Virgin internet have never caused me any problems that couldn't be resolved, so I've stuck with them; I rarely make UK calls so BT works for me. For international calls, Alpha Telecom has been consistently cheap and reliable over the BT line. It's not the cheapest at 3p a minute to France, USA and Australia, but it works for me and, man, does it have a sexy electronic voice when you dial in! 1899.com and 18185.co.uk are a couple of cheaper, slightly more androgynous, alternatives.

SAVING £100s

www.thisismoney.co.uk/cheaper-phone-calls
www.alphatelecom.com/uk
www.1899.com   www.18185.co.uk

Consider a pay-as-you-go mobile

Ask yourself this: is your mobile phone absolutely necessary?

If the answer is yes, then ask yourself whether you really need all those minutes and texts that come as part of your package. If you hand over £50 a month to your mobile phone company, that's £600 a year – or around £800 of your gross salary. If you have a full-on, show-off phone you can pay twice that over the duration of the contract.

fwiw*: If you're earning a salary of £20,000 and you pay £100 a month to your phone company, bion* you are working for almost a month just to talk and text cr*p. How gr8* is that? bwl*, <3.

Have you forgotten that you can buy a pay-as-you-go phone for as little as £30 and only pay for the odd call as and when you need to? Or try this: arrange to meet your friends and then just show up. On time. If you're l8* and your friends have gone, go and do something else. It worked for people for thousands of years. <3

*GLOSSARY: fwiw: for what it's worth; bion: believe it or not; bwl: bursting with laughter; gr8: great; l8: late; and <3 is a heart on its side to indicate love and affection, a condition that many people seem to share more with their phones than people.

SAVING £100S

www.thisismoney.co.uk/cheaper-mobiles
www.thismoney.co.uk/philosophy-of-the-phone

8 Learn the art of shopping

If you buy food, keep it in the fridge for a week then throw it away, congratulations! You are a living failure.

Harsh but, come on, is there really anything more moronic than buying stuff to feed your bin? Daytime reality TV, maybe. But apart from that? The Government has kindly worked out that individuals are throwing away £420 worth of food every year – families, more than £600. That makes no sense, other than to prove the influence that marketeers and spin doctors have over our decision-making processes.

Food shopping forms a significant part of our monthly outgoings. And the supermarket is where the bulk of the money is spent. Tesco takes £1 in every £8 spent by UK shoppers. But be warned: stores spend a fortune studying how to make us part with more of our money than we intend to. Have you ever wondered why your favourite song is playing in the background as you navigate the aisles? Have you even noticed the background music? Possibly not, but you will have noticed at the checkout that the bill is often more than expected.

For heaven's sake don't buy ready chopped fruit and veg – you only need a knife to start saving money on this one. Similarly, buy loose fruit and veg rather than "saver" packs. Although the packaged items can sometimes work out cheaper, ask yourself whether you'll be able to eat it all before it goes off, which often isn't very long – or whether you even want that much.

The supermarkets aren't all bad. They will usually, helpfully, display the cost of items (in tiny print) in uniform measures such as per 100g, 100ml or per dishwasher tablet. It's a great way to compare, but beware, they'll get you on the way round the store by placing cheaper products on lower shelves, making them harder to see, and again at the checkout with racks of sweets and other devilishly tempting offers. Be hard on yourself. You don't need sweets.

They'll also place the must-have items such as bread at the far end of the store to make you walk past EVERYTHING else on the way, and place items they really want you to buy at eye level. Hat's off and all that, they're brilliant at making you buy more than you intend so make sure you never go shopping hungry or thirsty – at least you can eliminate one level of temptation yourself.

In order to win this game of retail brinksmanship hands down, simply make a shopping list. Dig out the cookery books, plan a few meals and only buy what you need.

Oh, and don't forget your carrier bags! Increasingly, stores are charging for the privilege and if you drive to the supermarket you can keep a supply in the boot.

SAVING £10 a week = £520 a year, £20 a week = £1,040 a year

www.thisismoney.co.uk/supermarket-watch
www.lovefoodhatewaste.com

9 When was the last time you went to market?

Why do supermarkets have the fruit and veg right by the entrance?

Could it be so you put it in your trolley first, squash it as you go round the store, throw it away the moment you get home, then repeat the process while buying yet more stuff you don't want?

Whatever the reason, one way to beat the supermarkets – that is, to eat healthily for less and not accidentally buy Pop Tarts because they're on a 2for1 – is to use your local market stall. Lower overheads should mean lower prices.

One supermarket trick is the half-price fruit punnet. They'll sell strawberries for "half price" at £1.99. But go to your local market and you will find the same sized punnet for £1. That, if you know your four-times-table-based division, is a quarter of the price.

SAVING £100s

www.thisismoney.co.uk/calculators

Consider own-brand goods

10

In spite of the rain, which was one of the reasons blamed for massive food inflation in 2008, you can still get a tin of supermarket own-brand baked beans for less than 20p and a loaf of bread at Asda, Tesco or Sainsbury's for around 30p. Enough said.

Admittedly, this is 30% more expensive than before the weather took its toll and before the rising cost of oil threatened to turn bread into one of life's luxuries. But it still makes for a cheap dining experience if money is one of the most important ingredients.

That doesn't mean you should forget the tricks that the supermarkets' marketing sorcerers play to magic money from your pocket into their tills. They'll lure you in for a tin of pre-cooked haricots in tomato sauce and you'll come home with your beans plus a three-pack of 3for2 organic sweetbreads, oh, and a nice new telly for the spare bedroom.

Remember, too, that some of that cheap bread has roughly the same nutritional value as a packet of paper clips and a stapler. Sometimes it is worth paying more for quality food if you can afford to. Check out the Real Bread Campaign.

SAVING £100S

www.tesco.co.uk   www.thisismoney.co.uk/caring-consumer

www.asda.co.uk

www.sainsburys.co.uk

www.sustainweb.org/realbread

11 Do you really need designer labels?

Celebrities are given expensive clothes to wear. You're not.

At the end of the day, and let's face it, you may only wear the outfit once, can you justify paying hundreds of pounds over the odds because a top designer has had his or her name sewn on the label? And can you honestly say you can tell the difference at a distance between a £900 Prada or Gucci bag and a £9.99 one from the market? Think about it.

Alternatively, if you must follow every move of the celebrity culture and just have to have the clothes, then check out asos.com, a website that sells cheap replicas. You can even select items by the celebrity's name.

Better still, why not get into more down-to-earth "slebs"? While you may have a secret admiration for all things Posh Spice, she's an expensive Los Angeles-based act to emulate: there are people a lot cooler than that. Bluesman Seasick Steve and TV's wildlife presenter Kate Humble spring to mind with their at-home, at-the-ranch, on the plains, on the railroad simplicity that mere normal people can aspire to – and afford.

SAVING £100s

www.prada.com

www.gucci.com

www.thespicegirls.com

www.seasicksteve.com

www.katehumble.com

www.asos.com

www.thisismoney.co.uk/money-savers

"Home life ceases to be free and beautiful as soon as it is founded on borrowing and debt."

HENRIK IBSEN, NORWEGIAN WRITER, DRAMATIST AND POET

12

SELL YOUR CLUTTER – OR GIVE IT AWAY

If you watch the kind of TV that helps people get to grips with why on earth they have an entire landfill site's worth of clothes they never put on, then you'll probably have heard the statistic that women wear only 20% of their wardrobe 80% of the time.

If that sounds like you, take this quick test: You're at home. Open a cupboard. Look inside. If it's full of clothes you haven't worn, or "good ideas at the time" you haven't used, for, let's say, three years – you don't need them. So why not sell them to someone else who does? There are plenty of people out there who want secondhand telescopes and second-rate fitness equipment.

In case you've not heard, eBay, the online auction house, has opened individual sellers to a world of buyers. And you can flog anything for the cost of a small commission. And believe it, you can sell – and people will buy – anything! Newcomers should consider buying a few items first to build up a rating as a respectable eBayer before starting to sell. And Freecycle is an international network of likeminded people who advertise stuff they no longer want with a view to giving it away to someone who does.

Whichever you choose, make sure you understand the value of your clutter – you may have a treasure trove of collectibles. Check the antiques books at the local library for prices.

SAVING Will depend on what's in your cupboard and loft. Use the income to reduce your debts.

www.ebay.co.uk
www.uk.freecycle.org
www.thisismoney.co.uk/ebay

13 Use your talent to earn extra cash

Let's face it, if you're not a pop star by the time you reach your 20s you're never going to be.

A country and western star, maybe, but there's not much call for those over here. Why is that? In 2007, according to one set of statistics, country star Garth Brooks, born 1962, became the biggest selling solo artist in history, beating Elvis Presley.

If you do play the guitar you may be able to use your talent to teach other wannabes the rudiments of rock, the 12-bar blues or the country two-step. In fact, whatever skill you have could be an opportunity to share your knowledge and earn extra money.

In the first instance, try approaching your local adult education centre. If they are interested, or you are apprehensive, they may be able to start you off with a one-off, one-lesson session to see how you get on. If you're more serious about teaching as a career check out your options at the Training and Development Agency (TDA).

SAVING It's not unreasonable to charge £20 as a private guitar teacher. One hour, once a week, is more than £1,000 in a year in the bank.

www.tda.gov.uk
www.thisismoney.co.uk/make-money

Do DIY –
but do it properly, please

14

We're a nation of obsessive DIYers but according to a made-up statistic, 98.57% of us are rubbish at it. Especially all men.

Instead of pretending you know what you are doing, why not do the whole shelf-putting-up and building-a-two-storey-kitchen-bathroom-extension thing properly. For around £100 you can take a course at your local adult education college to improve the skills needed to tackle most household repairs. If the college runs plumbing courses you could soon be on track to wiping out the costly call-out charges and extra insurance policies once and for all.

Once you can tackle the basics of carpentry, you can create all manner of unique features and furniture using recycled materials. Decking made from recycled oak is a fabulous alternative to the bog-standard offerings in DIY stores.

There are "How to" guides all over the internet, including videos at VideoJug and printed guides in newspapers such as *The Guardian*. But remember: Please don't ruin your house/marriage/life by being idiotic, overambitious or leaving jobs unfinished. You may find yourself exposed for such crimes on daytime reality TV and no one wants that. Do they?

SAVING £100s

www.tinyurl.com/make-a-bench (Guardian)
www.videojug.com/tag/diy-house-and-garden
www.thisismoney.co.uk/diy-investing

15 Shop around for the cheapest home insurance

Unless you drive – car insurance is mandatory – you don't have to have insurance. You certainly don't need to get breakdown insurance for your toaster but for some things it's strongly advisable.

Can you afford to foot the bill if your house burns down? Probably not. Similarly, can you afford to pay over the odds for the same policy available elsewhere because you can't be bothered to shop around? Possibly, but it's not advisable.

One of the enduring elements of greatness about the Web is the engines that make finding cheaper insurance so much easier than it used to be. You can compare hundreds of policies in minutes, read the small print for catches and see what extras are available at what price. Extras such as emergency cover for burst pipes, for example, can be a good thing at the right price if you have old pipes.

SAVING £100s

www.thisismoney.co.uk/insurance-finder

Understand your travel insurance

16

If you are going on holiday abroad you should seriously think about taking out travel insurance.

If you're lucky enough to possess basic common sense you won't be taking the family jewels to the beach so all you're really interested in is medical cover. And in Europe that is already available at the same level that applies to each country's citizens – either free or at a reduced cost. To qualify you need to get a European Health Insurance Card (EHIC), formerly the E111. If you are a worrier or going skiing or are travelling outside the EU, travel insurance is a must. You can pick up a quality one-week European policy for a few quid and a year's worldwide policy for a family for way less than £100.

But if you have an annual policy that is about to expire and you don't have a holiday booked, DON'T renew the policy. You're handing your money over to cover an eventuality that won't happen. You wouldn't have car insurance if you didn't own a car. Simply restart the cover again the next time you book a trip.

AUTHOR'S NOTE After the national humiliation that was the opening of Terminal 5 at Heathrow airport, you should check the small print of your policy for baggage cover. Bags go missing with alarming regularity. Did you know that an estimated 800,000 laptops go missing or are stolen at airports across the world every year; 900 of those from Heathrow every week!

SAVING £100

www.thisismoney.co.uk/travel-insurance-finder
www.nhs.uk/EHIC

17 Choose cheaper breakdown insurance

When times are hard one of the things we cut down on is getting the car serviced. Or if the car was never a necessity and money is now tight, the chances are you'll be using it a lot less. Both of these actions can increase the chances of a breakdown. A pump seized up through lack of use can be just as bad as a timing belt that should have been replaced a couple of months ago. Now is the time to take a look at breakdown insurance.

The sector is dominated by big names such as the AA and RAC. But being towed home if your car breaks down is just another form of insurance like any other and there are scores of cheaper alternatives.

Check first that you cannot add this cover to your car insurance policy. Some offer it as an add-on for a reasonable fee.

SAVING £100

www.thisismoney.co.uk/breakdown-insurance

Are you paying too much for your life insurance?

18

We're living longer. Still going to die, mind, but as a result the cost of insuring the unthinkable is getting cheaper all the time.

If you were sold a policy when you took out your mortgage you may have been under too much stress to shop around. You could be missing a trick.

So what is the trick? If you are looking to make sure your mortgage is paid off if you die, this is one type of insurance where the cheapest is the best. It's called term assurance. You can find it at brokers such as Cavendish Online or by contacting companies individually.

If you don't have dependents or you don't have a mortgage you don't need life insurance. If the worst happens there'll be no one to benefit from any payout.

SAVING £100s

www.thisismoney.co.uk/life-insurance
www.cavendishonline.co.uk

19

BOOK YOUR HOLIDAY EARLY

Not long ago the advice for booking a holiday was the complete opposite. You waited till the last minute and took your pick from the hundreds of holidays the tour operators couldn't shift.

But low-cost airlines put an end to that. By selling the first few seats on each flight incredibly cheaply, they created a market for people prepared to travel to any destination that was cheap enough.

The concept was so popular that the whole travel industry began to adopt the first-come, first-served pricing model, with the best deals available only to those who booked early. According to the travel agent Trailfinders you should book 11 months in advance for the best long-haul prices. Remember, only a few seats on each flight are sold from the bargain basement. The crunch may change that and there is evidence to suggest that cheaper seats are available for longer, but there is unlikely to be a major policy change.

The weaker airlines will simply go out of business and the stronger ones can ground their aircraft until things pick up. While this pricing practice remains, airlines and tour operators would rather send planes out empty than go back to the old ways. So book early.

SAVING £100s, depending on the size of your family and where you are going.

www.easyjet.com
www.ryanair.com
www.trailfinders.co.uk
www.thisismoney.co.uk/tourist-rates

20 How to find cheap flights

When flight comparison services first appeared online it was revolutionary. Suddenly you had access to the same computer systems that travel agents did. Instead of relying on a desultory 16-year-old behind the desk of a High Street shop with no customers on weekdays and only enough chairs to allow for three customers at a time on Saturdays (closed Sundays obviously), you could suddenly sort the whole thing out yourself whenever you liked. Brilliant.

But as the big companies gradually woke up and came online and a plethora of sites started up offering similar services, the revolution was over. Now if you want to find the best prices you need to check a bunch of websites, which have different deals with different suppliers.

When booking flights always remember to check the websites of national carriers – BA, Air France, SAS, and so on – because they often come out cheaper than the flight comparison sites and the "low-cost" alternatives, especially if the dates you want to travel aren't flexible.

SAVING £100s

www.skyscanner.net

www.expedia.co.uk

www.opodo.co.uk

www.ebookers.co.uk

www.lastminute.com

www.travelsupermarket.com

www.kyak.co.uk

www.holidayextras.co.uk

www.bookingwizz.com

www.orbitz.com

www.travelocity.co.uk

www.cheaptickets.com

Lest we forget Teletext

21

Once upon a time anyone looking for a bargain holiday would spend hours in front of the Teletext pages on ITV waiting for each page of fuzzy writing to load up with special offers from travel agents, whom you would then telephone to make a booking.

Then the Web came along and it was, well, kind of the same, but different. In fact, one of the best websites was the Teletext flights service, which showed every flight going to every destination with every price. That was removed. Teletext refused to say why but presumably it was too transparent and the airlines complained. "A commercial decision," no doubt.

The game became to see if you could book your own package cheaper than the agents. If your holiday consisted of flights, accommodation, transfers and possibly car hire you'd order a brochure from a leading holiday company and work out the price of your holiday including all the complicated supplements. Then go online and, starting with the flights, try to put the same package together. You can still do that and win but the market has matured.

Teletext and the agents that advertise through it fought back with a vengeance and now the deals provided by the traditional travel agents can prove unbeatable once again. Not only will you end up talking to a person, which can be a huge relief now that there are so many travel sites that you need to check, your holidays are ATOL protected, which means if the holiday firm goes bust, you get your money back and they bring you home.

SAVING £100S

www.teletextholidays.co.uk   **www.thisismoney.co.uk/travel**

22 Change how you think about holidays

If you are feeling the pinch but can't bear the thought of cutting back on travel – and most of us will agree the last thing we want to lose (after the work laptop with the customer data on) is our holiday.

We do that going-to-work-every-day thing for all those weeks, we deserve a holiday or three. Don't we?

If this sounds familiar, stay fewer nights. Choose seven instead of 14 nights. It may sound obvious and, no, one week won't be half the price of two weeks but there are daily expenses on holiday that we tend to ignore but keep on adding up.

If you want to make the biggest savings, think about staying away for just two nights – or even one. A one-night off-season stay in a UK campsite in a tent will cost maybe £3 all-in. You can't say cheaper than that. Two and three nights and you can still pay using the change in your pocket.

The point about holidays is not about finding the absolute cheapest but getting away from the day-to-day grind. Do it right and after one night away, if you pack enough in, it can feel like you've been away for a week.

SAVING £100s

www.thisismoney.co.uk/savvy-travel

Learn to say "no"

23

It's easy to capitulate to the demands of a screaming child in a packed toy shop on a Saturday afternoon. But don't do it. You're the parent. They're your rules.

And neither you nor your child needs a giant plastic toy replica kitchen with nearly real-looking bananas and a miniature extractable ironing board in your lounge, even if they are crying themselves sick about it in public.

Similarly, but hopefully without the kids, how often does a "swift half" after work turn into a £50 drinking session with a quick curry you can only remember when you see your bank statement?

And those stag/hen nights you keep being invited to that end up being long-weekends in places you'd never heard of until Ryanair flew there, and none of you really want to go to but no one dares say so?

Sound familiar? So say "no".

Saying "no" a few times a year will do wonders for your bank account. And people that matter will respect that.

SAVING £100s

www.thisismoney.co.uk/credit-crunch

24 How to avoid expensive days out

Lastminute.com was one of the great early dotcom brands, one of the great survivors – and one of the great mysteries. You can book flights and holidays months in advance. What's last-minute about that?

It does, however, have some fine last-minute deals for things such as London's theatres and the nation's theme parks. Up to 50% off for top shows is not uncommon and a family can easily save £50 on a day out at Chessington World of Adventures, Alton Towers and the like. It is worth signing up for the site's newsletter to keep up to date with the offers.

But *the* place for consistently good offers for London's West End theatres is the famous "half-price ticket booth" in Leicester Square. Unsold tickets are available for half price every day from 10am and if you're not too fussy about the show you'll always find a bargain. You can check availability every day at tkts.co.uk. If you are fussy about where you sit, however, check out the wonderful Theatre Monkey for its seating reviews.

In case you've forgotten, an awful lot of museums offer free admission these days and they've come a million miles from the boring, stuffy old institutions they once were. And did you know that if you join the Art Fund – membership fee less than £50 for a family – you'll get free entry to 200 fee-charging museums, galleries, historic houses and castles across the UK and half-price entry to most major exhibitions at the major national museums.

SAVING £100s

www.lastminute.com	www.theatremonkey.co.uk
www.tkts.co.uk	www.artfund.org

Beat the ticket touts

25

Ticket touts earn their living by getting hold of tickets that are "otherwise unavailable". Well, here's the news: they are available to everyone when they first go on sale. You just need to know when they go on sale. Simply sign up to the free ticket alert newsletters from the main agents to ensure that you're first in the queue. Try these:

SEETICKETS The first choice for discerning concert-goers. It often holds back seats to give those people unable to log on first thing in the morning a chance of getting a ticket.

TICKETLINE A lesser known Manchester-based agency that often has tickets after others have sold out.

STARGREEN A real gem because even fewer people have heard of it.

TICKETMASTER INTERNATIONAL Why not think about travelling further afield? The venues in other countries are often smaller than in the UK so you get a better view and the tickets can be half the price. Worth considering if you want to make a weekend of it.

GIGANTIC This is worth a look too if your tastes are bit more eclectic.

Don't forget to sign up also for alerts from your favourite artists' and the venues' websites. If anyone knows when a tour is being planned you'd like to think it was the artist or where they are playing.

SAVING £100s

www.ticketline.co.uk	www.stargreen.co.uk
www.seetickets.com	www.gigantic.com
www.ticketmaster.nl	www.thisismoney.co.uk/tickets-rip-off

26 The cost of keeping up appearances

Through modern history, TV sitcom has drawn on characters from suburbia to ridicule the idea of trying to outdo the neighbours.

The weaknesses of these characters was perhaps best encapsulated in the 1990's BBC comedy *Keeping Up Appearances*, which featured the hilarious attempts by Hyacinth Bucket – pronounced "Bouquet", she insisted – at climbing the social ladder.

Trying to keep up appearances is little more than a costly illness. It's called snobbism.

A snob, says the dictionary, is someone who "vulgarly admires or imitates those of superior social position or wealth and looks down on those he considers inferior". Meet Mrs Bucket.

Remember, you cannot judge someone by what they have because you don't know how they got it.

Chances are they're in more debt than you are.

SAVING £1,000s

www.thisismoney.co.uk/get-out-of-debt

"Money can't buy friends, but you can get a better class of enemy."

SPIKE MILLIGAN, COMIC ACTOR AND AUTHOR

27 Trade down your car

So, you bought an American sports utility vehicle (SUV) that nets 15 miles to the gallon, on a whim.

Obviously we're all very impressed – especially by the personalised number plate, leather seats that heat your bum to whatever temperature a bum needs to be in a car, twin-screen DVD system with Sat Nav, CD and all the other trimmings that make a trip to the supermarket more comfortable.

But, seriously, can you justify the ongoing expense? If not, get rid of it. Then visit a car supermarket such as Cargiant, where you can choose from thousands of cars at knock-down prices. If you're a true money saver, consider an ex-rental model, which you can pick up for a fraction of the cost of a new one.

Rental company Avis sells its used cars direct to the public for 50% off list price. It claims you will save £1,000 off a dealer's price and most cars are no more than six months old. And visit Honest John, a former used-car salesman, for a colossal round-up of advice, reviews and discussions on buying used cars.

SAVING £1,000s

www.cargiant.co.uk

www.avis.co.uk

www.honestjohn.co.uk

www.thisismoney.co.uk/car-insurance-finder

www.thisismoney.co.uk/buying-a-car

Dump your car altogether

28

Have you ever thought about whether you need a car at all? In other words, have you ever sat down and worked out how much it is costing you every month?

In the real world, until a reliable beaming machine is invented to transport us and our families from A to B by disassembling our molecular make-up and firing us to wherever we want to go with pinpoint accuracy via the sweet shop (maybe that's what the Large Hadron Colliders will do eventually?), a car is pretty much the accepted alternative.

But it is worth taking a look at the maths. If you have a new car on finance and drive 30 miles a day to work and use it at weekends for mucking about and you're young enough to have hatefully expensive insurance premiums, it's not unreasonable to expect to pay £500 a month for your car. (£250 finance, £150 petrol, £100 tax and insurance) That's £6,000 a year or £18,000 over three years. Not so long ago you could buy a flat for that. It may well end up being the case again.

You can find out the ongoing costs of owning a car with the RAC Cost of Motoring Index. It takes a range of cars and lifestyles to show the, sometimes shocking, weekly outlay.

SAVING £1,000s

www.rac.co.uk/web/know-how/owning-a-car
www.thisismoney.co.uk/car

29

WALK OR CYCLE TO THE STATION/ WORK

It maybe a bit of a hippy notion to many people but – wake up and smell the floodwaters, dude – the hippies were right and whichever way you want to look at this, walking is free.

Without getting too biological, the average human being walks at about three miles an hour. That may sound slow compared with a car but it does mean you can walk half a mile in 10 minutes and a whole mile in 20.

According to the Department for Transport, the average commute by car across Britain is only 8.7 miles. And in London, figures vary, the average speed of traffic is but 10–12mph. You can cycle at between 10mph and 15mph. You work it out.

Cycling, if you don't count the cost of the bike or the fluorescent paraphernalia and puncture repair kits, is also free. There's certainly no parking charges for bikes. And there are generous tax breaks available if you cycle to work. Sadly, there is a long way to go in Britain before cyclists, motorists and pedestrians grow up enough to tolerate each other on the same street. And only a change in the law will sort that one. But they've done it in Belgium. There's even a free AA-style breakdown service for cyclists in Belgium.

Oh dear, that's Belgium mentioned twice already. But if Belgium can do it...

SAVING £100s

www.cyclenetwork.org.uk
www.sustrans.org.uk
www.visitbelgium.com/bike.htm
www.thisismoney.co.uk/tax-free-cycling

30 Ask yourself: Do I really need this?

Imagine the scenario.

It's lunchtime and you've got an hour to kill. You find yourself in a department store and there's a sale on. You pick up a beautifully packaged selection of barbecue tools and associated garden accessories and: "Oh my god! Is that a terracotta chiminea?" You've always wanted an authentic Mexican patio heater. And it's half price.

Now, stop! Ask yourself: "Do I really need this?"

"Do I really need this in my flat? Do I really need garden equipment and a ludicrously expensive, fragile outdoor conversation piece in my one-bedroom attic flat that doesn't even have a garden?" Exactly. Put it down. Walk away.

If this scenario rings even only partly true, apply the "do I really need it?" rule to every potential impulse buy, especially in the supermarket. You will start to appreciate and value things in a way you could never have imagined.

Not only will you save a fortune but you'll also find the inner peace you so desperately crave. That will lead you to love and a lifetime of happiness. After a couple of years, you'll move in with your partner and find a house with a picket fence and a private garden blessed with the sweet smell of jasmine. Now you can go and buy your patio furniture and that foreign heater thing.

A more realistic scenario, perhaps, is to step back and think. When you see a pair of jeans or shoes that look exactly like the kind that would suit you, is it because you've already got six pairs just like it at home?

SAVING £100s, maybe £1,000s.

Get off the station before your usual stop and walk

31

Yep, walking *was* already covered a few pages back but this is about more than one-foot-in-front-of-the-other.

It's about sticking two fingers up to the railway companies and the prices of their journeys. It's about changing your habits and as a result your outlook. And though the theory can be applied to any city, with the appropriate infrastructure, it's mainly about London and an underground system with a reliability that makes foreign visitors stare in bemused awe at the blank arrival boards and a Circle Line sometimes so ineffectual that one suspects it must be a Square with trains unable to negotiate the right-angles.

As commuters well know, London's transport system is divided into zones. What you may not know is that if you have a season ticket that takes you only as far as Zone 2, you can still use buses in the central Zone 1 at no extra cost. And what you may have forgotten is that central London isn't very big and you can walk across much of it easily in half an hour or less. Avoiding adding Zone 1 to your season ticket can save £100s of pounds – even more if you can lop off a station at the other end by walking a bit further or cycling.

We may be creatures of habit but isn't it worth tinkering with the routine if it's costing more than £50 a month in unnecessary fares?

SAVING £100s

www.livingstreets.org.uk
www.thisismoney.co.uk/discuss-rip-offs

32

CUT DOWN YOUR DRINKING

Circa 2008, our pubs have been closing at a rate of five a day! While there's a small amount of irony in the fact that pubs set up in converted closed-down bank branches are now closing because of the credit crisis, it is a tragedy for publicans and their families.

The smoking ban has taken its toll, of course, and food and drink inflation hasn't helped. There's also been a trend for pubs to refuse entry to anyone who cannot show photo identity to the big man in the tight suit guarding the door. It doesn't encourage conviviality.

So without wishing to alienate those fine people in the pub trade it is, with a sheepish sense of regret, worth noting that a few beers after work a few nights a week can be a financially debilitating state of affairs and you should set limits and stick to them.

If you drink at home, as more people clearly are, and you drink a bottle of £5 wine a day, that's a £1,825 a year – enough to make serious headway in any debt-reduction plan. Or try this tip from a French connoisseur: instead of buying cheap wine often, buy one top-quality £20 bottle once a fortnight. You'll not only save money but will start to appreciate and learn about the art of wine and wine making.

AUTHOR'S NOTE If you think you have a drink problem, believe it or not you can get hypnotherapy to stop drinking after a certain number of pints. Or for £10 you can buy the excellent book, *Beat the Booze*, which is an easy-to-read stab at highlighting and solving drink problems in their various guises. Check out too the *Drink Aware* website, which has a range of advice including a list of excuses you can use to refuse a drink without causing offence.

SAVING £100s

www.thisismoney.co.uk/pleasures-v-treasures
www.beatthebooze.com
www.drinkaware.co.uk

33 Smoking kills – it says so on the packet

Never mind the guilt, the smell, the health implications, the fact that it has become illegal in most indoor places and the cowering in a sorry back alley outside the office in the rain, a couple who each smoke 20 cigarettes a day are in the habit of sucking away £4,200 a year between them. Stick that in your Isa and (don't) smoke it!

If the returns on investments return to, well, returns, and you were to invest £4,200 a year in a fund that netted a modest 6% a year, after 20 years you'd have £160,000 to play around with. That's better than being dead, last time I checked.

If you enjoying smoking that's fine but read that last paragraph again one more time. At current rates, if you retired with an extra £160,000 in the bank, it would buy you a subscription to Sky Sports for 480 years, perfect for a happy, healthy – if rather longer than normal – time in your twilight years.

SAVING £1,000s

www.givingupsmoking.co.uk
www.thisismoney.co.uk/funds
www.thisismoney.co.uk/savings-calculator
www.thisismoney.co.uk/financial-health-check

Cancel your gym membership

34

The growth in the number of gyms opening over the last few years appears to be matched pound for pound with the growth in number of obese people. Work that one out while you workout if you will.

Could it be because most people are paying for membership and not going? Preferring to eat instead? Or is it because the only people who go to gyms don't need to go because they're already so damn fit that normal-sized people take one look and run a mile?

Whatever it is, if you pay your £50-odd a month by direct debit and kind of forget about the cost but you use the gym three or more times a week, great. If you're only using it once every two months it's costing you 100 quid a go. Think of all the cake you can buy for that. The point is, if you're not getting your money's worth, cancel your membership immediately. You'll soon save enough to buy your own bike and, if you're so inclined, a rowing machine. You can get a perfectly adequate motorized treadmill at Argos for a couple of hundred pounds (four month's gym membership). But do remember that if you cancel your membership because you're strapped for cash and you give notice in the middle of the month, you'll likely have to pay the following full calendar month's fee before it expires. They've thought of everything.

Consider running home from work now and again. It's free – provided you don't have a celebration pie, chips and beer binge when you get home.

SAVING £100s

www.runnersworld.co.uk
www.thisismoney.co.uk/fit-finances

35 Use your library

The local library should be a mecca for the money saver.

If there is a good library in your neighbourhood use it. You'll never need to buy another cookbook, guidebook or, oh the irony, lifestyle manual again and if you can bear to wait a few weeks in the queue for the latest blockbuster, you never need to buy books again. If they haven't got the book in stock, they'll order it for you from another library. Or they'll give you a login so you can order it yourself from your home computer. At whichbook.net you'll find a website that allows you to find a book and check if it's available at libraries across the country.

You can surf the internet, they run reading groups, hold story sessions for children, art exhibitions – some even rent toys and paintings. Nowadays you are even allowed to talk out loud without being shot down verbally by the crabby old rat-people that libraries used to employ to make misery for bookworms.

If you still aren't convinced, imagine something you've always wanted to know about, go to the library, they'll have a book on it and you can learn about it. The book is an unimprovable format. And almost all of the above is FREE.

AUTHOR'S NOTE The library also acts as a fascinating cultural barometer of modern Britain. The most popular books of all time, other than dictionaries and religious tomes such as the *Bible* and *Koran*, include: *A Tale of Two Cities* by Charles Dickens, *The Lord of the Rings* and *The Hobbit* by JRR Tolkein, *The Catcher in the Rye* by JD Salinger, *Charlotte's Web* by EB White, *The Tale of Peter Rabbit* by Beatrix Potter, *Harry Potter and the Deathly Hallows* by JK Rowling, *To Kill a Mocking Bird* by Harper Lee, *Black Beauty* by Anna Sewell and *The Godfather* by

Mario Puzo. But none of these writers feature in top 10 lists of authors borrowed from our libraries in 2007/08. These days we are are reading: James Patterson, Jacqueline Wilson, Daisy Meadows, Josephine Cox, Nora Roberts, Danielle Steel, Ian Rankin, Mick Inkpen, Janet & Allan Ahlberg and Francesca Simon.

If you're not familiar with these names, it's time to visit the library to see what the fuss is all about. Everyone else is in the know. It's time you caught up.

PS. You get fined if you take books back later than the agreed date. There's always a catch. But if you're extremely late taking a book back you can offer to buy it.

PPS. Don't stop buying books. That would be a silly idea for all sorts of complex philosophical reasons to do with what you're reading right now. But a paperback book is a much better investment than a glossy mag full of ads. Paying money for adverts… think about it.

PPPS: Once books go out of copyright – the authors are long dead and don't need the money – you can download them for free from the awesome *Project Gutenberg* website. There are around 3 million books downloaded a month from a catalogue of 25,000 titles – not only the classics in English, but also foreign and audio books.

SAVING £100s

www.whichbook.net
www.gutenberg.org
www.thisismoney.co.uk/bookshop

36 Beware the **3**for**2** trick

Down-to-earth people will understand that a special offer is designed to tempt you into buying something that you wouldn't otherwise buy. They will ask why, for instance, if something is now 50% off, were they trying to make us pay twice what it was worth in the first place?

But we live in an age of marketing gurus and professional spin doctors who have perfected in laboratories ways to extract every last penny and ounce of common sense from previously sane people.

There is something to be said for buy-one-get-one-free deals if they pass the "Do I really need this?" test and another "Was I going to buy this anyway?" test. Not forgetting the "Have I bought more food than is needed for the number of meals I'm going to eat this week?" test. But then there are the three-for-twos: a particularly cynical way stores entice shoppers to buy not one or two but three things they don't want – often perishable items. Every year, families throw away more than £600 of unused food. And campaigners such as Sustain, the alliance for better food and farming, lay the blame for that at the shelves of supermarkets that display these tempting "go on, buy more" offers.

Go shopping armed with a clear head and keep the enemy of spin in vision at all times.

SAVING £100s

www.sustainweb.org
www.thisismoney.co.uk/eat-well-for-less

Buy clothes in the sales

37

The advent and rise in popularity of online video and picture-sharing websites will ultimately mean that every single photo and movie clip ever taken in history will be uploaded and searchable.

And that, for me, is a terrifying prospect. Not because too many of my social misdemeanors have made it on to celluloid but because with a few clicks of the mouse, it will be patently obvious to anyone bored and lonely enough to search for images of "Richard Browning dress sense", that at every wedding I have ever been to in my adult life I was wearing the same suit.

One suit? That's enough isn't't?

OK, I'm lucky I don't have a public-facing job and I'm really not qualified to comment too much on suits but I've seen the posters on the suit shop windows. Normal day, nice suit, cost: fortune. Sale day, nice suit, cost: hardly anything. As the sale continues, the posters get bigger, the suits get cheaper and by the end staff are running out into the streets to hand suits to passing scruffy people they feel could do with tarting up.

Buy clothes in sales. There you go. That's all I was trying to say.

Oh, and don't buy clothes in the sales that you're only buying because they're cheap and that you will probably never wear.

SAVING £100s

www.thisismoney.co.uk/savvy-shopping

38 Play the Christmas lottery

The easiest way to cope with Christmas is to start a letter with "Dear Santa", and then send him the whole Argos catalogue. Sorted. You'd never have to buy anything for the rest of your life.

But it doesn't work like that. That's why we must thank God that Father Christmas makes all those toys for free. Imagine how expensive Christmas would be if we had to buy them.

Then there are the friends and relatives.

Instead of trying to buy a present for every relative in your family, consider getting together beforehand and picking one name from the hat. You then determine a price limit and buy one thoughtful gift for your chosen recipient rather than attempting to please everyone at considerable cost.

Everyone gets a present, everyone saves money.

Or why not send your partner a love letter as a present this year? Thoughtful, meaningful, and free.

SAVING £100s

www.thisismoney.co.uk/christmas-money

The National Lottery – it won't be you!

To better understand the lottery try this game with a friend.

■ Find a field and enter – a football pitch will do.
■ Take a marker pen each and place blindfolds over your eyes.
■ First player spins round a few times till dizzy then walks around the field for five minutes before randomly selecting one blade of grass, which he marks with the pen. First player then leaves the field.
■ Second player repeats the move as above and also marks blade of grass.

Rubbish game right? But imagine that the two players miraculously both selected exactly the same blade of grass from the millions on the pitch. That's about the same chance as you have of winning the lottery jackpot. In fact, the odds of winning the main UK National Lottery are stacked 14m to 1 against each ticket. Statisticians will tell you that it can take up to 300,000 years before the numbers on a £1 ticket come up.

Some highly organised syndicates buy 14,000 tickets a week, which reduces the odds to 1,000 to 1 – but that's no guarantee of a win. For the rest of us, the difference in the odds between buying, say, 10 tickets and one is insignificant.

If you have to gamble, limit yourself to one ticket. Or consider the Premium Bonds from National Savings and Investments, at least that way you never lose your stake, which you can cash in at any time. And you could win £1m.

SAVING £100s

www.nsandi.com
www.national-lottery.co.uk

www.thisismoney.co.uk/lottery-calculator
www.thisismoney.co.uk/best-cash-isas

40 Use your Isa allowances

Time was that putting spare money in a bank or building society account was about the most sensible way of saving for a rainy day – or all summer as it's now known. Experts recommend an easy-to-access nest egg of three to six month's salary as back-up in case we lose our jobs.

The way banks have been collapsing, that advice now looks rather shaky. Provided you do your homework –and don't just do what you're told by a mate who's found a great rate in some dodgy bank you've never heard of – your savings of up to £50,000 (at the time of writing) are covered by a Government guarantee. And the Government isn't going to go bust any time soon – is it?

Before you choose a savings account, check who owns the bank to which you are entrusting your cash. If you intend to split your savings between banks that are owned by the same "parent" bank, the £50,000 limit applies only once. So if you are lucky enough have £60,000 saved in two banks owned by the same parent, which then went bust, you'd lose £10,000. You can see a full list of who owns who at www.thisismoney.co.uk/safe-savings.

Remember, you can save up to £3,000 a year in a cash Isa (for the more financially savvy there's also a stocks and shares Isa). You don't pay tax on the interest accrued so, if you have spare cash in your current account, this is the difference between earning next to no interest and up to around £150 a year.

SAVING £100+

www.thisismoney.co.uk/best-savings-rates
www.thisismoney.co.uk/long-term-savings-calculator

Claim your benefits and tax credits

41

There was once a certain stigma in Britain attached to claiming benefits. Well, not any more. The Government has put benefits at the heart of the family budget and it's your money so make sure you're claiming it. Even newborn children are now given a benefit in the form of the Child Trust Fund (CTF) the moment they're squeezed screaming from that nice warm womb.

Unfortunately, some of the newer benefits have been so complex that they either remain unclaimed or are incorrectly assigned, which can result in people on low incomes having to pay money back. And doubly unfortunate, some of the most needy in society – elderly people – still believe it is wrong to claim what is rightfully theirs because of the old-fashioned stigma topped up with pride. They forget they've have paid for it in advance over the years.

But there is help out there. And in the first instance, that can come from you. Once you've made sure you are up to speed with your own Child Benefit, Employment and Support Allowance, Working Tax Credit, Child Tax Credit, employee-related tax benefits, Housing Benefit and any free prescription entitlements, make sure your gran or any elderly friends who trust you are also on the case. Citizens Advice (formerly the Citizens Advice Bureau) is free and there's a simple one-page guide on its website to all the benefits available. Everyone should take time to peruse it. Otherwise pop down to the local branch.

SAVING £100s

www.adviceguide.org.uk/benefits
www.thisismoney.co.uk/ctf
www.thisismoney.co.uk/ask-an-expert

42 How saving £50 a month now can save you £120 next year

As anyone who has read the Bible will tell you, money lenders were plying their trade more than 2,000 years ago.

So when people of a certain age holler at you: "Don't buy what you can't afford! Save up for it first, like we had to," you have to ask for how many people that was really true. And how far back in history do we need to go to find a time when money or its early equivalent wasn't being lent? Never, I suspect. These do-gooders also forget that if you want a university education these days you have to pay a considerable amount of money for it and students are increasingly beginning their careers with massive, unavoidable debts. Anyway, harking back to these possibly mythic good olden days, this tip is nevertheless based on the "if you wanted something you saved up for it first" rule but reworked for something we tend not to think about – even though it crops up every year. And if you drive a car is unavoidable. Insurance.

QUESTION Do you pay your insurance premiums by monthly installment?

If you do, then consider this: you could be paying a premium of between 15% and 20% for the privilege. So, if your home and car insurance bill for the year is £600, you're paying up to £120 a year in interest by paying monthly. If you can save up for next year's premiums in advance, you can save the cost of any interest by paying the whole lot in one go.

SAVING £100+

www.thisismoney.co.uk/car-insurance-finder

Do you need all those TV channels?

43

The switchover from analogue to digital TV has started and is due to be completed by 2012.

You only have to take a trip to the local tip to see the piles of old tellies that tell the story of a nation that has already invested heavily in newfangled sets. In fact if you want further evidence of this, one of the reasons our inflation figures remained low when the prices of food and oil were rising so fast was because, it was claimed, the prices of flat-screen TVs had come down so far, so quickly.

If you still haven't sorted your digital TV and you want to watch the box you're going to have to take the plunge and choose a provider. The choice is bewildering and with telephone, internet and mobile-based services running in tandem as all-in packages you need to think hard about what you want and what you can afford. Do you really need – and are you really going to watch – every sports and movie channel, which can cost well in excess of £50 a month, £600 a year? Remember Freeview, as its name suggests, is free.

Some Freeview set-top boxes, such as those made by Humax, act as personal video recorders (PVRs) that allow you to pause and rewind shows you are watching, or record programmes while you are watching another channel. Or that Tiscali TV has the largest selection of on-demand television series, films and music in the UK? Sky and Virgin are not the only options.

SAVING £100+

www.thisismoney.co.uk/digital-tv   www.humaxdigital.co.uk

www.digitaluk.co.uk   www.tiscali.co.uk/tv

44 Bin the ready meals

There have been so many learn-to-cook-food-properly shows over the years that there is no excuse for not getting stuck in yourself.

The king and queen of the genre have to be Delia Smith and Jamie Oliver. Delia got people hooked showing that by following a recipe precisely, anyone can cook and Jamie Oliver took it to another level with the idea that here's the basic recipe, now experiment. Both brilliant. But both with a lot of work still to do – because people are still buying ready meals.

Look: assuming you have some seasoning and other basics in your kitchen, to make your own really simple shepherd's pie you only need potato, meat and a tin of tomatoes. To make your own apple pie all you need is flour, marg, sugar and three apples.

Ready meals may be convenient, but preparing your own food saves money and can often be quicker than faffing around with three different packets and a microwave. A visit to your library will reveal loads of books dedicated to cooking proper meals in less than 30 minutes. Try to get hold of the classic *Cooking in Ten Minutes* by Edouard de Pomiane. It has a version of every conceivable dish you can make in 10 minutes.

SAVING £100+

www.abebooks.co.uk   www.thisismoney.co.uk/healthy-eating
www.deliaonline.com
www.jamieoliver.com
www.thisismoney.co.uk/bookshop

Avoid the payment protection racket

45

Do you want insurance with that? *This is Money* has campaigned hard to expose the sharp practices of the finance houses flogging expensive and inappropriate payment protection insurance (PPI). Never heard of it? Well, check your statements as you may have a policy without even realising.

It was several years ago that we first warned that banks and other lenders were adding this largely pointless, overpriced rip-off insurance to loans in an underhand manner. Later, the official money watchdog, the Financial Services Authority, agreed and you may be able to get your money back.

Banks aren't thieves, that's nonsense. But they worked hard to make customers spend £100s on an insurance that is supposed to maintain your loan repayments if you lose your job. It was an insurance people simply didn't need or want.

The problem is that for many people, when you come to claim you find that you cannot. Stories include people who are off work for months after serious surgery who discover that the insurance only covers the minimum interest payments on their credit cards rather than anything worthwhile.

If you have been sold a policy – and you may not even be aware of it – you should dig out any paperwork from your loans and mortgages, check the figures and the small print.

SAVING £100+

www.thisismoney.co.uk/protection-racket
www.thisismoney.co.uk/ppi

46 The extended warranty trap

Electrical goods are more reliable than ever.

Think about it: how many times has your fridge broken down in the last five years? And do you really need the hassle of claiming for repairs to a £15 toaster?

If your new radio won't last three years then perhaps it's not worth buying in the first place. Yet stores will try to sell you a policy costing £5 for portable radios that cost as little as £18 – that's nearly a third of the price.

There comes a time when you just have to cut your losses and buy a new one if it breaks down, which it probably won't.

Remember, warranties are just another form of insurance and when sold at the till like this are a nice, easy earner for the retailer. If you feel you may need protection, thank the retailer, sleep on it and check with an insurance broker for a policy. For more expensive items, it's more than likely that when the manufacturer's warranty runs out, they'll send you an offer to insure it longer term anyway. Think carefully before you accept.

SAVING £100

www.thisismoney.co.uk/warranties-guide

Shop online

47

The internet is gradually taking over – and it's partly down to the weather. It's also because online grocery shopping is improving all the time and there are plenty of comparison websites to help find the best prices for bigger items.

Recent figures from UK retailers show that 17p in every pound is now spent online – 20 years ago it was zero – and it is expected that within five years half of all shopping will be done this way. The biggest growth areas have been in clothes as people search for ever-lower prices resulting from lower overheads.

It could prove devastating for the traditional High Street. Electrical stores such as Richer Sounds, which has a branch network across the country, are fighting back with guarantees to beat prices on the Web but there is no escaping the fact that people prefer to order from a computer screen when it's raining.

If you haven't taken the plunge yet, it has to be worth your while. There are no crowds of people to fight through, no queues at the till and placing a winning bid on an auction site can even feel quite exciting. Just remember rule number one: don't buy what you don't need.

Specialist search sites such as find-dvd.co.uk are an absolute must to visit if you want to see the cheapest suppliers – including delivery – of a particular title.

SAVING £100s

www.find-dvd.co.uk

www.kelkoo.co.uk

www.pricerunner.co.uk

www.ebay.co.uk

www.fixtureferrets.co.uk

www.richersounds.co.uk

www.mysupermarket.co.uk

www.shoes.co.uk

48

MEET YOUR NEW FRIENDS: CITIZENS ADVICE

If you are in debt, remember Citizens Advice (formerly Citizens Advice Bureau) is your friend. There are 3,000 branches across the country and if your debts are out of control please seek help immediately from your local CAB. It's a charity with advisers who can help you work out a sensible strategy to get you back on your feet. Other new friends you may want to get in touch with include the following charities:

CREDIT ACTION Aims to help educate people about how to handle money responsibly.

CONSUMER CREDIT COUNSELLING SERVICE (CCCS) Offers free advice and help to financially distressed families and individuals. Free helpline: 0800 138 1111.

NATIONAL DEBTLINE Offers a free, confidential telephone helpline for people with debt problems in England, Scotland and Wales. 0808 808 4000.

ADVICENI An agency for people in Northern Ireland that can put you touch with relevant charities. 028 9064 5919

BUSINESS DEBTLINE Debt advice for small businesses: 0800 197 6026

SAMARITANS Confidential non-judgmental emotional support, 24 hours a day for people who are experiencing feelings of distress or despair. 08457 90 90 90.

SAVING It could save your life

www.citizensadvice.org.uk

www.creditaction.org.uk

www.cccs.co.uk

www.nationaldebtline.co.uk

www.adviceni.net

www.bdl.org.uk

www.samaritans.org

49 Cut your own hair

Whenever former Spice Girl Victoria Beckham has a haircut the Google search monster goes into overdrive serving up results for news and pictures of the momentous event to a globe's worth of celebrity worshippers. "Dyer-no-wott? I'm gonna get one just like it."

Back in the real world, haircuts aren't that interesting. On a local scale, they rarely make the news. One exception, however, was when a leading High Street hair salon charged a six-year-old girl £35 for a five-minute trim. It was a revelation that should spur any parent into trying to avoid this kind of place.

In my world, while banks take your money and use it to make money for themselves, hairdressers take your money so they can talk at you about Spain while making your head look like diseased topiary. But one thing these industries have in common is that when, all things considered, you are charged more than you would expect to reasonably pay for a product or service, you've been ripped off. Surely it would be a reasonable assumption to make, that a haircut for a six year old would cost a fiver. OK, maybe a tenner if they bother to wash it. But £35?

It's not like you need proper training to become a hairdresser in this country. Anyone with a pair of scissors or £20 clippers from Amazon can call themselves a hairdresser. So can you. Go on have a go. You could save £100s and don't worry ... it'll grow back.

SAVING £100s

www.thisismoney.co.uk/money-savers

Take up a money-saving hobby

You're halfway through the book. Well done so far. And now for the most important tip of all: get a hobby. If you are at all musical, artistic or show signs of talent in any direction and are not following it up you are committing a crime not only against yourself but against other people whom you could inspire.

For one, if you can immerse yourself in a task for hours it will give you limitless amounts of pleasure for possibly little or no cost – after an initial outlay in equipment. And the benefits of not spending money on expensive alternatives such as going to the pub are massive.

Hobbies not only open your mind to new experiences but they can introduce a new world of interesting like-minded people.

If you need to see some financial justification let's imagine that a painting takes 20 hours to complete and you'd normally be out getting through a pint of beer an hour in the pub in your spare time. That's a saving of a least 40 quid a picture. If you then sell a painting you're even earning money from your hobby. Think about it. The savings really start mounting if you are spending weekends with your hobby rather than on city breaks in Dubai.

Get painting. Go fishing. Grow tomatoes. Make a stained-glass window. Write a book. Do something. Anything.

Thank you for listening.

SAVING £1,000s and £1,000s

www.thisismoney.co.uk/money-chat

Take a packed lunch to work

It's obvious. So obvious in fact that years after publishing an online money-saving guide that omitted the packed lunch tip we still get emails from around the world suggesting it as one of the great "no-brainers".

"Do the maths, guys!"

So here goes: you spend a conservative £5 a day on lunch plus the luxury of £1.50 on a coffee and £1 on snacks, it's nothing. It's only £7.50 a day. Or £1,800 a year. Or, for the hard of understanding, the cost of a brand new £10,000 car after a mere five years.

Over your working life you can easily chomp away more than £100,000. And you know what? An awful lot of people spend considerably more than £7.50 a day. While making your own lunch isn't free, remember: a sandwich is just some bread with some stuff in between. And for the price of a small pension, does the coffee really taste that good?

To really benefit, try to eat breakfast at home before leaving for work. It will help cut down on the mid-morning snacks, which can easily turn into a £500 annual habit.

SAVING £1,000s

www.thisismoney.co.uk/eat-well-for-less
www.thisismoney.co.uk/money-savers

Buy in bulk

52

If you have caught the cheap-lunch bug and are in habit of making packed lunches or feeding a family and you have the will-power not to stuff your face with the whole 50-pack box of Monster Munch like you're in training for the UK heats of the International Crisps Eating Olympics, then buying in bulk is a winner.

It varies, but one pack of crisps costs around 45p. A six-pack, £1. And it's £2 for a sack.

But take note: in spite of what you may read out there, you cannot successfully freeze a decent sandwich with salad. You can freeze cheese and ham sandwiches but if you really don't have enough time in your life to place a slice of ham between two slices of bread you seriously need to consider seeking specialist help. It takes a lot longer to thaw a sandwich, for heaven's sake.

Here's a trick for bulk buying. If you are not loyal to a particular supermarket, think of the product you buy that costs the most money – coffee or washing powder, maybe. Then go to the website Mysupermarket.co.uk. Search for the product and you'll be able to see which store, if any, has it on promotion. Go to that store this week, buy a big supply of it and do the rest of your shop there. There's always the danger that you'll be tempted by all sorts of other things that you don't want, especially if you're in a shop you don't normally go to, but we've already established that you have will-power. Right?

SAVING £100s

www.mysupermarket.co.uk
www.thisismoney.co.uk/savvy-shopping

53 Use quality low-cost clothes shops

Blimey. Have you *been* to Primark?

No? Then imagine a giant ants' nest that's been stamped on by a naughty child and the ants are rallying around desperately trying to pick up all the pieces by dragging them around in sacks and bagging them up for transfer to a better place.

The one in London's Oxford Street at any rate is a vast emporium of perfectly good-quality clothes at prices so low that there's an element of disbelief amid the excitement that steams off the thousands of shoppers as they binge on bargains.

TK Maxx is another one. An upmarket jumble sale of last-season's designer wear – and sometimes this season's – where you'll find clearance bins with name-brand shoes down from £90 to a fiver if you're really lucky. As the crunch hits the mainstream retailers increasingly harder this will be the place to go for even more unsold fashions than usual.

SAVING £500+

www.tkmaxx.co.uk
www.primark.co.uk
ww.thisismoney.co.uk/deals

Use quality low-cost food shops

In 2007, after four decades on the British high street, pile-it-high sell-it-cheap supermarket chain Kwik Save went bust. If only it could have held on for another year.

The low-cost supermarket model has now officially arrived in the form of Lidl, Aldi and Netto and with the current squeeze on consumer spending it is bedding down rather successfully.

The big four supermarkets, Sainsbury's, Asda, Waitrose and Tesco, will be keeping a close eye on proceedings. Research by consumer group Which? found that customers could save up to 20% by shopping with these newcomers. And they're looking to expand. At the time of writing, Netto even has a page on its website, pleading for landowners to get in contact if they have suitable plots for sale for its stores. Aldi has also announced an expansion drive and Lidl is growing.

Their sales pitch of lower prices without compromising on quality is proving a hit with cash-strapped families even if the shopping experience isn't as convivial as the established rivals. A tendency to offer larger pack sizes can present people who live by themselves with a dilemma but if you are a discerning money saver, check them out.

SAVING £100s

www.lidl.co.uk
www.aldi.co.uk
www.netto.co.uk

www.thisismoney.co.uk/money-shop

Avoid the car wash

The credit boom helped create a corresponding boom in sales of new cars with a knock-on boom in the hand car-washing industry.

Every urban car park seemed to have one. And every one seemed to have a queue of drivers willing to part with up to £40 [some were more than £100] for a Gold, Silver, Platinum or Titanium wash. How clean does a car need to be?

Maybe it's a pride thing. Whatever the psychology, it is money down the drain.

Washing your own car wash will cost pence in electricity to power the vacuum cleaner and heat the water. The water and cloth (old T-shirts, if you're not having to wear them) are already paid for and the free exercise is a bonus.

Unfortunately, and tempting though it may be, not washing your car at all is not a great idea. Dirt can encourage rust, and rust speeds up the process by which your car goes from 60 to 0 – thousand pounds, that is.

SAVING £100s

www.thisismoney.co.uk/car

Reclaim your bank charges

56

It's not often that Britain's ineffective watchdogs throw their weight around enough to justify their existence. But there was an exception in 2007.

The Office of Fair Trading ruled that banks had been overcharging customers for years. So, if in the past six years your bank manager has charged you for an overdraft or made you pay for one of their hateful automated letters, you had officially been ripped off and could claim back your money.

Some of our readers were receiving cheques for more than £20,000. The banks, however, weren't happy and fought back with an appeal, which at the time of writing is still to be heard. The advice is to still go ahead and make your claim and let the bank sit on it until a ruling is made. In some cases, banks have been paying up anyway.

If you're worried that your bank has now been nationalised and that your claim will somehow be a burden on the taxpayer, remember if it is decided that these charges were illegal, you have not only the law on your side but the knowledge that it was always your money and you're entitled to have it back.

Claiming involves a bit of rigmarole with bank statements and interest calculations. Use the link below and follow the instructions - we've made it as easy as we can and if you're owed £100s or £1,000s – it is worth the effort.

SAVING £1,000s

www.thisismoney.co.uk/bankcharges
www.thisismoney.co.uk/reclaim

Reclaim your mortgage fees

If you have redeemed your mortgage in the past four years or so (it depends on your lender), the chances are you've been overcharged in the form of an elevated exit fee.

Lenders used to charge around £50 if you paid off your mortgage either because you were clearing it for good or because you were moving to another lender. From around 2004 they started to increase the fees, some to as high as £300.

This is when money watchdog the Financial Services Authority stepped in and ruled that there was no justification for such high administration fees. You can get your money back – the difference between what you paid and what you should have paid, that is. Tens of thousands of people already have.

Obviously, lenders aren't thieves. But they have made another administrative error here and if you could get back up to £220 for one phone call, wouldn't you?

SAVING £100+

www.thisismoney.co.uk/reclaim

Credit card tarts may look sweet but...

58

"Card tarting" is a technique where, if you are incredibly organised and money-savvy, you can theoretically take on the credit card companies at their own game. It centres around the 0% interest phenomenon that began several years ago – and even now there are people who will tell you there is mileage in playing this game. Beware.

If you owe money on your credit cards, you're already a victim – trying to transfer your debt is merely putting off the inevitable. When you come to take out a new 0% card, you could find you are either turned down completely or offered a low credit limit. You will instantly face a punitive interest rate from which there is little, if no escape.

Credit card companies aren't stupid. They want their money back and will charge as much as they can. If you have a history of credit card problems, cut the cards up. Certainly don't take out more. Ever. You could save yourself £1,000s and avoid a lifetime of financial misery.

If you fall for these kinds of games, you may also have fallen for the store card trick. You're at the till, they throw in a line about "signing up for our store card will save you 10% off this purchase." They don't mention that the interest you're charged if you don't clear the balance is almost as bad as it gets – up to 30%. Say no and consider shopping elsewhere in future.

SAVING £100s

www.thisismoney.co.uk/credit-card-reality-check
www.thisismoney.co.uk/store-card-misery

59 Sort out all your finances in eight steps

So far this millennium, the right-thinking person will be forgiven for thinking that the financial services industry has gone a bit deranged; staffed by greedy imbeciles and liars who use jargon as a smokescreen for huge commissions and PR subterfuge to cover for borderline crimes.

Since 1999, *This is Money* has tried to see through the spin and to make sense of the whole thing with clear, easy-to-understand news, tips, advice and analysis of the industry and what it means for you. We have hundreds of guides to everything you ever need to know about your money.

But it took an American cartoonist to turn the complex world of finance into a simple eight-point 129-word plan of action that could work for most people. Actually it was nine but number 4 doesn't exist over here.

Scott Adams, creator of that perennial office politician, Dilbert, wrote the Unified Theory of Everything Financial. You will need, he said, a house, a pension, a will, some savings, investments, debt-free credit cards and life insurance. And number eight: if you don't understand any of this stuff, pay for advice.

It may sound like pure common sense to many but that's what has been missing these last few years.

SAVING well, that depends

www.dilbert.com
www.thisismoney.co.uk/8steps

Pay for your prescriptions in advance

If you're ill and facing a hard time financially, you really don't want to feel the need to cut back on medication because you can't afford it.

There is, however, a little-known but top money saver for those who need regular prescriptions – the ability to pay in advance. It's like a subscription for all your prescriptions.

Patients who have to pay for more than three items in three months or 14 items in 12 months will find it cheaper to buy a pre-payment certificate (PPC).

The downside is that unfortunately it will be those people in the worst health who benefit most from this scheme. So get well soon and don't forget, of course, to check if you are entitled to free prescriptions, which you can do on the PPC page of the website below.

SAVING £100s

www.ppa.org.uk/ppa/ppc_intro.htm
www.thisismoney.co.uk/heath

Grow your own herbs

In American they pronounce herbs, "erbs". In normal circumstances, our cultural, regional and national variations in pronunciation should be something we need to respect, nurture and protect.

But "erbs"? Come on! It's like the nation is so utterly devoid of culinary pride that they can't even be bothered to utter the whole word of one of the most important ingredients in nice food. "But yer cain't fry a chive, y'all."

The point is, and there is one, growing herbs may seem like a trifling thing so let's put it in perspective.

Any self-respecting cook will use a lot of herbs and if you're happy with dried ones, fine, this probably won't apply. But if you buy those pots from supermarkets, read on. Even if you only have a windowsill this is something you can do and find worthwhile.

It is quite easy, planting seeds at regular intervals, to set up a nice little production line throughout the spring and summer months. You could save up to £100 over the growing season. More if you have a garden or allotment.

PS. If you are lucky enough to travel to the USA, check out the Souplantation & Sweet Tomatoes chain, you can get all-you-can eat fresh salads, pasta, soup and pudding for next to nothing. It's brilliant.

SAVING £100

www.thisismoney.co.uk/caring-consumer
www.souplantation.com

Neighbours: don't try to beat them, meet them

62

How often have you nipped to the DIY store for a power tool or a new ladder to fit a couple of screws and light fitting?

Or how often can you honestly say you have used that brand new sewing machine you bought on a whim? Your neighbours may not only have what you need, but they will be usually delighted to be asked to help. You can easily save £100 a year.

Maybe, it was something to do with a certain Australian TV soap that cheapened the meaning of the word "neighbours" and resulted in people, particularly in the South, having a relationship with the people next door that extends to little more than a nodding or grunting acquaintance.

Talk to them. They might even be nice. It's how friends are made. And money can be saved.

SAVING £100+

www.thisismoney.co.uk/money-chat

63 How to choose a builder

Poor old builders, eh?

Time was, you had a dripping tap and the plumber would only come and fix it if you agreed to a whole new kitchen, bathroom and central heating system. That, or the call-out charge and half-hourly fee meant you suddenly became the proud owner of the world's most expensive faucet. (The name turns posh when they get that dear.)

Now things are different. The work has dried up and although the prices are still going up the rules stay the same.

Try to only ever use a builder who is personally recommended by someone whose opinion you trust. If you're new to the area, meet your neighbours and ask them.

Remember, a decent builder doesn't need to advertise and won't. You could save £1,000s and avoid a skip-load of potential misery.

If you are worried about bursting pipes, check your home insurance to see if you can add it as extra. Once water starts leaking, it never stops until you get it sorted.

SAVING £1,000s

www.thisismoney.co.uk/cost-of-home-improvements

Make do and mend

64

The sad reality in these green, carbon-neutral days is that you can't repair a toaster. Or most other things, for that matter.

There's plenty of sympathy from retailers and the odd remaining repair shop but your only real option is to take your dead toast-maker to the tip and drop it in the recycling bin. If that's not possible, you'll have to chuck it and claim another little plot of landfill, where it can lie with the rest of the country's defunct gadgetry.

There are, however, things that you can repair or get repaired. Brick walls, car windscreens, furniture, your glasses, boiler, computer, washing machine, upholstery, your pride, confidence in the banking system. Stuff like that. But even a washing machine that has a few years under its belt falls into the "hardly worth it" category when you can get a new one for a couple of hundred quid and the repair may be more than half of that – and then it's only temporary because once things start to go…. It's a tough choice but don't just throw things away before checking the cost of repair. You wouldn't throw your car away because it wouldn't start one winter morning.

SAVING Face

www.wickes.co.uk
www.diy.com
www.thisismoney.co.uk/diy-chat

65 When it comes to fashion, sizes matters

There are worse things in your closet than that dodgy old skeleton waiting to emerge in front of the in-laws when you least expect. And worst of all are the clothes you've never worn.

At least with skeletons you know, hopefully, that you had a fun time somewhere down the line. Unworn clothes on the other hand merely tell the story of a loser. Someone who went shopping and lost.

You need to ask yourself why you have clothes that you haven't worn? Because, you see, there is no point.

If it's a mental health issue please, please get help, but in the meantime learn how to hire the clothes for free. It works like this: buy whatever you like within reason, put it in the cupboard for a couple of weeks then take it all back. It's pointless but may help ease the problem.

A bigger concern is if you are buying clothes one or two sizes too small in the hope that you will lose weight in the not-too-distant future – once the diet and new exercise routine you haven't started kick in. Face it people. It ain't gonna happen. Is it?

SAVING £100s

www.weightwatchers.co.uk
www.mind.org.uk
www.thisismoney.co.uk/financial-health-check

Avoid the parking crimes – and the fines

66

There are approximately 6,600,000,000 people on this planet of ours. And generally speaking most of us are decent, upstanding human beings as we try to get along with our lives and our neighbours with goodwill and a fair spirit in our hearts.

And then there are traffic wardens. Or parking attendants. Or any number of other amusing names we could come up with. Anyone who has ever had a parking ticket will understand.

You pay your car tax, petrol duty, VAT, road tolls, congestion charge and obligatory insurance. You pay for tunnels and bridges and child seats and hand-free mobile sets and speeding fines. So don't pay for parking fines!

The best way to avoid fines is to make sure you park legally. It means you'll have to walk a bit further but is that such a bad thing? It's not always that easy when the goalposts are being shifted and the lines are redrawn every other week.

If you do get caught out by camera, by stealth, by accident or by uniformed officialdom and you believe you have been wronged – do all you can to fight it. There is a guide on *This is Money*.

SAVING £100

www.thisismoney.co.uk/fight-parking-tickets

67 Drivers: slow down and save

The Orwellian vision is almost complete.

A new generation of roadside cameras that track average speeds across swathes of Britain were announced in the late summer of 2008. Ultimately, it means our basic human instincts and judgment are being monitored every time we get in the car.

Unless you drive everywhere at 20mph it is becoming all-but impossible to avoid being caught speeding at least once in your life. Next step, presumably, will be fines for driving too slowly or having the wrong kind of face for the motorway.

There are now more than 6,000 speed cameras waiting to catch you out. You can find out more about them from the campaign group, The Association of British Drivers (ABD). The safest and only way to beat them is to slow down – and there are financial benefits from doing this.

If your driving involves high mileage here's something to think about. According to the Department for Transport, driving at 80mph instead of 70mph can use up to 25% more fuel. That means if you drive 10,000 motorway miles a year, that's a saving of around £350 just for sticking to the limits.

SAVING £100s

www.thisismoney.co.uk/car
www.abd.org.uk

Avoid the motorway service station

68

When the first motorway service station, Watford Gap, opened on the M1 in 1959, people reportedly used to drive there for a day out. Now, these places can feel like they're merely the world's most expensive toilets.

Coffee up to £3 a pop, cash machines that charge a fee to withdraw your money, petrol that costs an extra tenner to fill the tank. It's not like they're on prime housing land – they're on the motorway.

If you travel a lot you should fill up with petrol before you go and take a flask of coffee; a bit old-fashioned but you could stuff 10 quid's worth of motorway coffee in one of those. Avoiding these places, just twice a week, could save you £1,000 a year.

SAVING £100+

www.thisismoney.co.uk/discuss-rip-offs

69 Learn to use a computer – and to type

One of the great things about being human is that we can learn skills that fish can only fantasize about in the wildest of their three-second memory moments. Humans can drive cars, make atom bombs, brew lager, visit the Moon, but before we do any of these we have to learn a few basic skills.

Before we climb behind the wheel of a car we'll take lessons and pass a test. If you want to build an atom bomb you need to grasp the basics of particle physics before buying the ingredients on the internet. And if you want to make lager you need ... actually no, just buy it. It's not worth it. Or is it? And there's the rub. If we want to, we can accomplish almost anything with a few lessons and some practice.

So why the hell doesn't this logic apply to computers? Far more people spend their working lives at a computer screen than they do driving lorries and planning nuclear wars. Yet almost no one knows how the damn things work. To compensate, companies spend fortunes setting up technical back-up teams, employing monkey people who can't communicate on a one-to-one level but happen to have read a couple of pages of the manual. And have an X-Box. Who are the monkeys now?

At the very least we should all: learn to type (online or by book), learn the keyboard shortcuts, learn the Google search tips, learn what all the options in the menu bar across the top of your various windows do. Be curious. Learn the right skills. Civilisation depends on it.

SAVING £1000s – time is money

www.thisismoney.co.uk/keyboard-shortcuts

We all make mistakes – don't pay for them

70

Businesses want your money.

It's a simple logic that, while obvious in the souks of the Maghreb, where they've been perfecting the art of luring tourists into carpet shops for about a billion years, is much more cleverly disguised in the so-called developed world.

Thankfully, most businesses, while they exist to make money, carry out their activities honestly and with dignity. But there's an underworld of scammers out there and you have to keep your wits about you at all times. Where a lot of people let themselves down is by not checking bills and statements properly – or at all.

Of course, we all make mistakes so it's important to see the good in people before challenging any bill. But you should always check your bank statements, restaurant and phone bills and till receipts. It's a chore to complain, and can be embarrassing if you're wrong, but those extras you never received at the restaurant, the mystery bank charges and any number of telephone and internet scams, could be costing you a fortune – and if you don't check you won't know.

SAVING £100s

www.thisismoney.co.uk/scams-chat
www.thisismoney.co.uk/top-10-scams

71

ANOTHER WAY TO GET CHEAP LONDON THEATRE TICKETS

The lure of the West End stage is a powerful one – and not just for the actors. Hundreds of theatre-lovers are bussed in from the provinces every day to watch, too often, over-priced dross. The price of the tickets alone is enough to cripple a family's budget, never mind the extra costs of transport, food and accommodation if you're travelling under your own steam. Much better value can be found in the fringe theatres, and even better, in small local or pub theatres.

If you must go to London, the Kings Head in Islington is highly rated, as is the Gatehouse in Highgate. The Soho Theatre, Royal Court, the Cottesloe at the National, the Donmar Warehouse and Peacock Theatre offer a happy middle ground. Outside London, the Theatre Royal, Windsor is a try-out venue for many West End shows. Theatres often email special discounts to registered users of their websites. Choosing yet another username and password can be a chore but it's a small price to pay for some great special offers.

If you have trouble remembering passwords, consider using the brilliant Password Agent that remembers them for you.

SAVING £100

www.thisismoney.co.uk/money-saving-days-out

www.moonsoftware.com/pwagent.asp

www.kingsheadtheatre.org

www.gatetheatre.co.uk

www.sohotheatre.com

www.nationaltheatre.org.uk

www.donmarwarehouse.com

www.royalcourttheatre.com

www.peacock-theatre.com

www.theatreroyalwindsor.co.uk

72 Use the internet (for things you otherwise wouldn't think of using it for)

Within the next five years, online shopping is expected to account for one half of all money spent in shops. Why not all of it?

If you're spending all your money in one supermarket you've already done your bit towards destroying the High Street. It doesn't take a huge stretch of the imagination, if everyone conspires, to finish off the town centre shopping experience for good.

You can buy almost anything online. And there are big savings to be had on things you may not otherwise have thought of.

Small electrical items, batteries, cables, leads and computer-related gizmos can be up to 85% cheaper than in High Street shops, which are having to compete directly with rivals based in Hong Kong. But it's not just small items. You can buy your new car, bicycles, TVs ... but did you know you can buy tyres online? Even if you don't buy, it's a fabulous research tool.

And if you're worried that you'll be out at work when your parcels are delivered, there's a service from Parcel Park that has a growing network of drop-off points around the country, where you pay a pound and collect later.

---

http://www.parcelpark.com
www.thisismoney.co.uk/online-shopping

Use charity shops

73

"Charity begins at home," Sir Thomas Browne wrote in 1642.

"Not any more it doesn't, mate. We're binge shoppers and it begins in the High Street, down the road from McDonald's and next to that really quiet estate agents and the newly closed down bank branch."

Charity shops have been a long-time feature of our town centres and when times get tough it can feel like they're the only things left. Here are a few tips…

BOYS If you only buy one thing from a charity shop in your life, make sure it's a tux. Tuxedos must be one of the great cons – a really expensive suit you wear only once or twice. It'll take time to find one the right size, but for the savings it's worth it.

GIRLS Perfectly good designer wear is hanging on rails waiting to be snapped up for a few pounds – you're doing something to help charity and helping yourself at the same time.

CHILDREN If you are in a play or assembly or a fancy dress party or need an overall for art, take your pocket money and your imagination to the charity shop. It's fun.

OLD PEOPLE Keep sending your stuff to the charity shops! Much of the clothing is back in fashion and highly sought after and a lot of that old tat is collectable. Thank you.

SAVING £100

www.thisismoney.co.uk/giving

74 Swap and share – books and more

Before money was invented, the currency of the people was barter.

You wanted a goat and you had a collection of Star Wars comics you'd find someone in the cave across the way with the opposite and you make the trade.

Later on, much later on, Noel Edmonds televised the process with a Saturday morning BBC1 programme called *Multi-Coloured Swap Shop*. That went on to spawn *Cheggers Plays Pop* – forget that – and even later, *Deal or No Deal*, a show about dangling money in front of contestants' faces then taking it away with one phone call – rather like banks, credit card companies and other lenders are starting to do.

Tenuous references aside, now there's a lot less money swilling around we could see a return to bartering. And for some things it makes sense, particularly if you've caught the recycling bug.

If you read a lot you should check out one of the book swapping services such as Readitswap it, which has more than 200,000 books waiting to be swapped. You only pay the postage.

SAVING £50

www.readitswapit.co.uk
www.whatsmineisyours.com
www.thisismoney.co.uk/noel-edmonds

Earn more money

75

Have you ever had one of those moments when you look at the guy down the road driving the fancy new top-of-the-range Mercedes and you think: "What on earth does he do for a living?"

The answer is likely to be: same as you. He's just taken out another couple of mortgages against the "value" of his house.

Judging by some of the cars jamming up Britain's roads anyone might be forgiven for thinking that the county is awash with cash. Debt, however, is not the same as cash.

Remember the figure: we owe £1.4 trillion - more than the economy itself.

If you need more money, one way is to get a second job in the evening or at weekends. However, the best way is to get paid more for what you do already. And the best and easiest way to do that is when you go for a new job. That might not be so easy in the current climate but it is always vital to try to negotiate more money before you start. If the idea of a second job is too horrifying, think about this: why not get a seasonal job? Christmas or other holiday work is not only temporary but it can be great fun.

An extra £1,000 per annum is extra every year.

SAVING £1,000+

www.thisismoney.co.uk/find-a-job

76

DRINK
TAP WATER

One of the many puzzles of modern life is why in parts of Africa people are dying because of a lack of water. Yet in Europe, the contents of a whole Alp in the environs of Evian is bottled up and shipped to the UK, where it rains so much that we can't wait to escape on the holiday we've booked – in Africa.

Bottled water! What a load of two parts hydrogen to one part oxygen – wrapped in plastic with a lid on.

Ok, if put to the test, you can taste the difference between different bottled waters. Part of that can be explained by the fact that some of it is basically tap water. But there is no doubt that some are smoother and some are more magnesium-y than others.

If you are a bottled water addict here's a puzzle for you: if you drink 1.5 litres of water a day – roughly the recommended daily dose for adults – and you satisfy this need with bottled water at 75p a litre, how much are you spending a year on water? Answer: £472.50. Turn the tap on folks. It's as good as free and in most cases it's as good as bottled.

If you've read the stories about oestrogen-like chemicals in plastic bottles, you'll probably be aware of the decent alternatives you can buy. But have you thought about filling your bottle and leaving it overnight in the fridge? You'll have a wonderfully refreshing drink to take to work.

SAVING £100+

www.thisismoney.co.uk/bottled-water

77 Make the most of your lunch break

Sorry folks, more maths. But read on, it's worth it.

If you work typically 48 weeks a year and have one hour a day for lunch, it adds up to 240 hours of spare time. If you normally work an eight-hour day, then your lunch breaks add up to the equivalent of 30 working days (a whole month) in which to do something worthwhile.

You can study for a new job, knit jumpers, sell stuff on eBay, write your novel – or, as a lot of people seem to do, wander round in a daze, buying shoes and sandwiches.

You choose.

Popping out and buying stuff because "there's nothing else to do" is a dangerous and expensive pastime and you will usually be buying things you don't need or even really want.

AUTHOR'S NOTE Readers should be aware that parts of this book were written and edited in breaks between my daytime job. If you put your mind to it and set aside regular time you can achieve anything.

As the world's richest man, investor Warren Buffett, said: "Life is like a snowball – all you need is wet snow and a really long hill."

SAVING £100s

www.thisismoney.co.uk/thisisnotwork
www.thisismoney.co.uk/warren-buffett

"For one person who dreams of making fifty thousand pounds, a hundred people dream of being left fifty thousand pounds. "

A.A. MILNE, WRITER

78 Cut down on the meat

As comedian John Cleese once said: "If God did not intend for us to eat animals, then why did he make them out of meat?"

Quite. But all that rearing can make meat an expensive luxury. While tradition tells us to think of a hearty meal as meat and two veg, by twisting the idea on its head and stacking up the plate with loads of veg with a little bit of meat on the side you can save a lot of money.

That doesn't mean making a mountain out of a 5lb pack of potatoes. It means being imaginative with swede and celeriac. But get it right and this is a cost-effective way of eating more healthily, which can only be a good thing.

A pack of meat may only cost £5 at the supermarket but a large head of broccoli is £1. Carrots are even cheaper.

Or how about going vegetarian from time to time?

It's easy to imagine that vegetarians spend most of their lives foraging for tofu and poring over science books for alternative ways of recreating the sausage. It's how basic prejudice is founded. Get over it.

There are an infinite number of recipes you can concoct. A baked potato prepared in the right way can provide the ultimate in easy, wholesome and cheap eating.

TRY THIS

■ Take your favourite vegetables, maybe a couple of courgettes and/or sweetcorn, an onion, a red pepper and a handful of grated cheddar.
■ Bake the potato with a little olive oil and salt rubbed on to the skin – start it in the microwave for six minutes to speed things up.
■ Fry the veg, slice the potato lengthways and scoop out the insides. Put it in a bowl with the fried veg and grated cheese, season with pepper.
■ Stuff the mixture back into the potato skin and bake in the oven for another 5–10mins.
■ Serve with a salad and a nice glass of wine.
COST £1 a head plus wine. Bargain.

SAVING £100s if you think like this often enough.

www.thisismoney.co.uk/cookery

79 Make the cheapest meal in the world for 10p

As any self-respecting subscriber to niche TV channels will tell you, there are people in the world who only have a bowl of rice to eat a day. And that is if they are lucky. This used to be the kind of information that only your mum knew about.

Today it's different. A fact, it seems, is only a fact if it was on the telly and the only people we can trust to impart dietary information are the presenters of daytime cookery programmes. After all, no one knows more about rice consumption than the ex-model who fronts World TV Channel 598's *You Are What You Can Only Afford To Eat*. In the last series, they mentioned the bowl-of-rice fact. So it must be true.

As the Western economy tip-toes on a knife edge, we all need to find more economical ways of eating. We're too spoiled to cope with mere rice. So here is the cheapest meal in our world that we may actually like: tomatoes on toast.

If you've caught the grow-your-own bug and have tomatoes ripe for cooking, pick them, dust them down and fry them in butter or olive oil. There are few greater tastes and smells than freshly picked tomatoes. Toast a couple of pieces of granary bread and spread with more butter. Sprinkle with brown pepper and serve. Get it right and the taste is exquisite. And at around 10p a serving it is one of the cheapest meals in the world. Even less than a bowl of rice.

SAVING depends on how often you want tomatoes on toast

www.thsismoney.co.uk/eat-for-less

" Where large sums of money are concerned, it is advisable to trust nobody. "

AGATHA CHRISTIE, AUTHOR

80

DO YOU KNOW HOW MUCH YOU SPEND?

Any financial adviser worth their salt – or any general busybody trying to help with your finances – will tell you to sit down and work out exactly how much you spend every day, every month and every year and compare that against how much you're likely to earn. "Work out a budget."

And that's fine if your finances are in meltdown. But if your money management is only slightly wayward you don't need to beat yourself up about it just yet.

A good way to start is to take a look at your past record and work from there. Start by digging out a couple of month's worth of bank statements and look for trends in spending that you can cut back on.

People who spend too much money often do so because they have absolutely no idea how much they're spending or what they are spending it on. If you notice a series of purchases on the statements in the same shop, stop going there.

Next step is to start keeping receipts. Keep a diary of everything you spend if you need to. Then at the end of the following month compare these with your bank statement, looking out for any more purchases, excessive cash withdrawals and even regular payments that you can't account for.

Once you've eliminated the unnecessary, if you're still arriving at the end of the month in the red, now's the time to get serious and work out the dreaded budget. Hopefully you'll be able to use the tips in this book to make savings without making misery.

SAVING £100s

www.thisismoney.co.uk/household-budget-calculator

81 If you buy magazines regularly think about getting a subscription

Buying magazines every week that you don't read is the same as buying food that you throw away, only this time you're starving your mind. To take the analogy a step further, there's plenty of junk out there so be careful to check first for artificial fillings.

Magazines are where we turned for specialist news and information before the Web arrived. But as the information online becomes harder to find and overrun by scammers and spammers, the magazine remains a trusted friend. Albeit a paid-for one.

This tip is to be followed only if you are sure you are going to read the magazine every time, all year! A magazine can easily have the same number of words as a novel so ask yourself first: how many books do you read a year?

The best tip is to ask for a subscription as a birthday present. Otherwise consider choosing one that comes out every other week such as *Private Eye* – less than £30 a year – or *Web User*, dearer at around £40, but packed with useful tips and tactics. Don't forget to check the subscription websites as well as the magazine's own site, and if you fancy brushing up your French, choose a subscription from Viapress.com, there's 1,000s to choose from and they deliver to the UK.

SAVING £50

www.private-eye.co.uk magazinesubscription.co.uk

www.webuser.co.uk **www.viapresse.com**

www.thisismoney.co.uk/reader-comments

Avoid the glasses rip-off

82

If you pop in to you local Toys R Us megastore you'll probably notice that you can buy a plastic house, with hinged doors, windows and a roof for less than £100.

Now cross the road and head for the optician. Here you'll find items made of exactly the same ingredients – plastic and wire – that are a tiny fraction of the size of a house yet cost twice the price. How do they do that? Could it be because it's a rip off?

According to the fellow behind online glasses shop Glasses Direct, a pair of specs that cost £7 to make, including lenses, are sold for £99 – a 1,000+% mark-up. If you have your prescription handy, you should consider using an online discount store, where you'll pay as little as £15 for a pair.

Wherever you buy your glasses, you do not need the hard coating, which should be an optional extra, although a lot of opticians no longer offer you the choice. You certainly don't need the anti-glare coating they are likely to try to sell you. The opticians was once purely a medical establishment but has evolved into a part-fashion accessory retailer so go prepared for the "hard" sell.

Of course, if you like your old frames – keep them and simply pay for new lenses. And don't forget to check out discount stores such as TK Maxx, which sells cut-price designer frames at some branches.

SAVING £50

www.glassesdirect.co.uk
www.thisismoney.co.uk/glasses

83 Avoid loyalty cards at all costs

The first rule of money is to hang on to as much of it as you can. You never know when you may need it.

The best way to do that is to SHOP AROUND. (Note: use of capitals to indicate use of the obvious). Loyalty cards, however, are designed to make you do the OPPOSITE OF THAT.

Loyalty schemes are devised by civilised society's worst enemy – people who work in marketing. The schemes usually come with a credit-type card to make you feel a little bit important and valued as a person. These are the kinds of tricks at the heart of marketing strategies.

The cards exist to make you spend more than you intended, to buy more than you intended, to be marketed (sold) things you didn't know you wanted because, in fact, you didn't want them. Never mind that they also act as yet another way of spying on your every move.

These schemes prey hard on your subconscious. In the back of your mind, every time you use the card it cons you into thinking you're somehow saving money as you accumulate the loyalty bonuses that will take you one step closer to the ultimate points nirvana. Which is usually a trip to the zoo.

SAVING £50

www.thisismoney.co.uk/loyalty-cards

Avoid cashback credit cards

84

The same psychology is at work for cashback credit cards as for loyalty cards. Only this time the rewards are even greater: FREE MONEY! Yes dear.

Clawing at your subconscious here is the idea that the more you spend the more money, free money, you'll get back. It's a brilliant concept for the card companies, whose sole aim is to get you into debt so you pay them interest every month.

Some cards offer 0.5% on purchases or £1 for every £200 you spend. Well, gee whiz swizz. Others offer up to 5%, which looks generous, but the amount you can "earn" is capped. And while the return of £360 over a year is a fantastically attractive notion, that's exactly the problem. To get it, you'll need to spend a whopping £7,200, 5% of which is likely to be over and above what you intended.

If you are incredibly disciplined and make regular payments using your credit card this can be a way of getting something back. But spending money in order to get a refund later is an upside down way of managing your finances and comes under the heading "trying to be clever". Why do you think credit card companies offer these deals?

Credit card companies aren't stupid. There is no such thing as free money.

SAVING £100+

www.thisismoney.co.uk/get-out-of-debt

85 Never take what you see on the internet at face value

Anyone can set up a website within a few minutes and the internet is awash with self-appointed experts in every subject imaginable. But beware the sites purporting to be money experts – they're lining their pockets not yours.

They'll be littered with ads, only you won't realise they're ads. They'll have financial "advice" that lures you into taking out the top-paying products. They'll pay Google for keywords to bring you to the website to make themselves look reputable.

Some take the form of directories that launch if you accidentally mistype your destination address. But many are cleverer than that, a lot cleverer. Especially the email-based scams.

No! You cannot win a lottery you have not entered. That African prince hasn't really got a fortune waiting to be transferred out of the country if only you'll hand over you bank details. And your real bank never emails (or phones) to ask you to confirm your details and your PIN number.

While you have to take your hat off to their ingenuity, for heaven's sake don't fall for it. Keep your wits about you at all times, otherwise you could quickly end up at the end of your wits.

SAVING £100+

www.thisismoney.co.uk/10-best-scams
www.thisismoney.co.uk/how-we-are-paid

Turn down the heating

86

A lot of rich people get rich because they understand the value of the pennies. We've all heard stories of the old guy who lived like a tramp in the freezing cold house, who used to reuse his teabags and who's revealed to have amassed a fortune when his will is read.

Here's a dumb statistic: If you reuse teabags, which cost around 2p each, and you drink five cuppas a day. Over 40 years and that's a saving of £912.50. It's also 73,000 cups of tea, half of which weren't very nice.

Similarly, you can get richer by saving 2% off your heating bill for every degree you turn down your thermostat and a further 10% if you turn it down to 10 degrees at night when you're cuddled up in bed with duvets and blankets. That could be up to £100 a year off a typical family bill.

Even if the statistics supplied by energy companies about turning down the heat are sometimes questionable, this thermostat thing is genuinely worth thinking about. £100 over 40 years is £4,000. Or 160,000 teabags if you prefer to look at it that way.

WARNING Don't turn down the heat too much. Prolonged exposure to cold can cause hypothermia and death, especially as you get older. There are grants and rebates and all kinds of free advice available from the energy helpline, Home Heat. If you have any worries please phone 0800 33 66 99 now.

SAVING £100

www.thisismoney.co.uk/cut-your-fuel-bills
www.homeheathelpline.org

87 Eat out for less – and help end the wine scam

We all know that restaurants will happily sell a £4 bottle of wine for £15 and more. But is that really such a rip off? With high rents, rates and other unseen costs these are businesses that need to turn a profit and marking up wine so we can eat well for less is probably acceptable. Not acceptable, however, is the increasingly virulent – and vile – habit of waiters rushing round the table filling wine glasses for you. And, oh, oh dear, I seem to have accidentally run out before filling everyone's glass on your table, would you like to buy another bottle? Don't put up with it.

One thing we should all do is ask, nicely, for a jug of tap water for the table. The *London Evening Standard* newspaper has been running a campaign to remove the stigma from asking for free water and it seems to be paying off. Waiters in the capital are now delighted to accommodate even if their bosses' stomachs are clenched.

If you haven't already done so, check out *Top Table* the restaurant website. It has a special section for half-price and other meal deals. It's well worth a visit if you can still afford to eat out – and you can book online. Or simply eat early. There are many ways restaurants try to lure early birds so they can increase the number of sittings and their profits. Pre-theatre menus are popular because everyone knows what time the table needs to free.

SAVING £100

www.toptable.co.uk

www.standard.co.uk

www.thisismoney.co.uk/bottled-water

www.thisismoney.co.uk/wine

How to save money on dental treatment

Good grief, my mother was right! The best way to save money on dental treatment is to avoid it.

No, that doesn't mean you can neglect your dental health long enough to qualify for a place on the Reality Teeth TV Makeover show. It means clean your teeth at least twice a day and eat fruit, not sweets.

A spoonful of sugar in your tea causes your teeth to decay for two hours. So, a cuppa every couple hours and you're going to be making regular contributions to your dentist's pension fund.

The longer you leave the business of looking after your teeth, the more expensive your dental bills will be when you're older and can least afford it.

SAVING £1,000s

www.thisismoney.co.uk/financial-health-check

89 Free guitar lessons

There now follows an utterly shameless plug for one of my favourite bands.

If you have always wanted to be a rock star but are either too old or can't afford £20 an hour for years of lessons there is an alternative courtesy of perennial cheeky boys The Toy Dolls, who boast one of rock's most talented unsung guitar heroes in Michael "Olga" Algar – probably because the band has remained unapologetically silly since they formed more than 20 years ago.

Go to their website and follow the links to Multimedia ⋯⋗ ⋯⋗ Guitar for a selection of eclectic video lessons from Bach's *Toccata* (part 1) to, um, *Sharon from Whitley Bay*, the classic *Nellie the Elephant* and the hilarious *Yul Brynner Was A Skinhead*.

If you want something a little less frenetic, *The Guardian* newspaper published a brilliant free *Learn the Guitar Guide*, which has been published online in full. That's free too.

SAVING £100s

www.thetoydolls.com
tinyurl.com/learn-the-guitar (*Guardian* guide)
www.thisismoney.co.uk/richard-browning (for more of my favourite music)

"Center Parcs" for half price

You either love Center Parcs or you hate it. It's the Volvo covered with Marmite of family holidays. If you've not been, think swimming pool with slides under a big domed roof on a housing estate in the woods. But if you can get over the mass check-in – an enormous very British queue where everyone quietly hates each other – you'll end up having a great time. The "parcs" somehow happily assimilate the masses and there is tons of fun stuff to do. But here's a weird thing. Most people, it seems, either swim in the pool, ride their bikes or watch the telly – all of which you can do at home. Weirder still is the fact that the parcs often seem to be fully booked – in spite of the cost.

A midweek Monday–Friday villa can cost more than £800 and more than £2,000 for a top-of-the-range "exclusive". Admittedly, it has its own own sauna, maid service, steam room, outdoor hot tub. It sleeps up to eight people so you can share the cost by taking your friends but this does make it, technically, the opposite of "exclusive".

Now then, if you are a little more adventurous you can nip over to Belgium and stay in one of their "Sunparks", for loads less. There aren't as many sporting facilities but there's the same pool complex, bike hire and big queue on arrival. The equivalent four-day break can be £1,000 cheaper for the big villa with the sauna, which sleeps not eight but 20. Different school holidays mean lower prices and fewer people. Even with petrol and Channel crossings it may make an attractive alternative if you need to cut back but can't face watching TV at home.

SAVING £100S   www.sunparks.be

Amazing free software

Google earns money from companies who pay for keywords that then appear as links on websites that display content deemed relevant to the keyword.

Every time their link is clicked on, the company pays Google – usually a few pence for introducing a potential new customer. But multiply those few pence by the entire globe and you have an enormous cash cow that has seemingly limitless funds to create incredible free stuff for us to play around with.

One such product is its picture editing software. If you find yourself struggling to sort your holiday photos with ill-considered proprietary software from your digital camera manufacturer or are loath to pay for a professional version then you should try the latest version of *Picasa*. It is brilliantly easy to use, especially for cropping, and it's free. Just make sure that you don't accidentally share your photos with the whole world if that's not your thing.

But as big and as liberal as Google may be with its freebies, it doesn't have anywhere near everything. There are thousands of amazing free downloads out there waiting to be installed to make life online easier, safer or more fun. Check out the fabulous *Gizmo's* tech support alert for a round-up of the best.

SAVING Possibly nothing, but a world of free stuff shouldn't be ignored.

www.techsupportalert.com
picasa.google.com
www.thisismoney.co.uk/holidays

Keep paying for music

92

"If music be the food of love..." and all that. If there is no music in your life, where's all the love that music conveys coming from? Music is not only the most popular and the most diverse art form – it's also the cheapest.

If you have internet access you can while away the days picking a genre and listening to every conceivable type of music on the music-sharing website YouTube, as people across the globe constantly upload new songs. Alas, not all of it is legal. Often the music being uploaded belongs to someone else and although YouTube has facilitated a removal tool for subscribers, you could be misled into thinking that copyright law no longer applies.

Because the music industry was slow in accepting and profiting from the possibilities that the internet offers, it has taken underground movements such as YouTube to shape the future.

It costs Google, the owner of YouTube millions of pounds a week and 10% of the world's bandwidth (the electronic juice that powers the internet) to allow users to watch, listen and enjoy all this music – at no cost to the viewer. But the artists aren't being paid either. Where such big money is at stake, hopefully the music industry and these modern-day publishers can reach a compromise that allows artists and their backers to receive just rewards.

Until that happens, keep buying your music because ultimately there's the danger that there'll be nothing of any note worth uploading.

SAVING Music

www.thisismoney.co.uk/best-music-download-sites

93 The DIY fixed-rate mortgage trick

Before the credit crunch there was a "cheap" way of creating your own fixed-rate mortgage deal without the fees normally associated with the lower-rate short-term deals. As the crunch ensued and previously unseen movements in interest rates began to occur, the banks saw it as a loophole and put and end to it. It is worth mentioning, however, because it was a way of shaving years off your mortgage and if things calm down it may well be possible to do it again.

Traditionally, mortgage lenders didn't charge a fee for their standard variable rate (SVR) loans because the rates were always higher than their fancy fixed-rate deals, which did incur a fee. But if you could find a lender that offered a low SVR and a flexible repayment plan it meant you could set your monthly repayments well above the minimum that was required. Fixing it yourself like this meant two things: one, if rates rose you wouldn't be affected because you were merely overpaying by less; two, if rates fell you would be saving even more. You can save thousands by paying off your mortgage early.

Unfortunately, because of the way the money system works behind the scenes, lenders found themselves with SVRs that were lower than their fixed-rate deals and began imposing punitive fees on these as well. Although no-one can say what the future of mortgage lending will look like. It is certain that banking will not be allowed to mess up so badly again. At least not until the generation of the greedy and stupid believe "it's different this time".

SAVING A hypothetical £10,000s – but you never know

www.thisismoney.co.uk/mortgages
www.thisismoney.co.uk/mortgage-finder

London Underground refunds

94

How ironic that we now have nationalised banks and a private railway.

While all things economic move in cycles, this is the complete opposite of how it used to be and the future shape of UK banking is in turmoil. If it turns out like Railtrack, our privatised then kind-of-renationalised railway lines, we'll end up with banks that are private companies limited by Government guarantee and regulated by the Department of Transport.

Critics of banking regulator the Financial Services Authority may prefer it that way. At least there's one benefit of private railways: individual companies have a charter that requires a certain level of service. If they fail to meet certain targets, passengers are entitled to a part-refund of their fares.

Each company has its own rules – so please check on the respective website. But one lesser-known refund policy is that which is operated by Transport for London (TFL), the body responsible for London Underground and Docklands Light Railway. It says: "If you experience a delay to your journey of more than 15 minutes, for reasons within our control, we will refund you with a voucher to the value of the single delayed journey."

At the time of writing, if your journey takes more than a quarter-of-an hour longer than it should, and even if the journey only cost £1.50, you'll get a £4 voucher towards future travel. And because you're dealing with a company plagued by knackered signalling equipment and a regular inability to finish engineering work on time, it soon adds up. Claim online at the TFL website.

SAVING £50

www.thisismoney.co.uk/tube-refunds

" A banker is a person who lends you his umbrella when the sun is shining and wants it back the minute it rains."

MARK TWAIN, AUTHOR

It's good to talk – no, it's vital

"It's good to talk" was an advertising slogan dreamt up by an agency on behalf of BT to make people make more phone calls. You can see it at Ad Slogans, the Advertising Slogans Hall of Fame, where you can also see such classics as "Access: 'Your flexible friend.'" – from the last time credit card companies turned sane people into over-indebted consumers.

Today, in some ways "It's even better to talk" because if you and the person you are calling have both downloaded an internet telephone program such as Skype – it's free. But advertisers don't want you to know about such inconveniences. They want you to spend, spend, spend. And if you spend too much, what do they care?

If the red bills are piling up on your mat, whatever you do don't ignore them. Even if you can't pay. Open them, read them, feel physically ill if you wish and if you cannot pay get in touch with the sender immediately and explain.

In spite of what you may feel and in spite of the images that advertisers convey of an unreal world to which you don't deserve to belong, banks, phone and gas companies are staffed by people just like you. And if you talk to them, and explain your difficulties, they can start to help. If you don't, they'll start what feels like a personal vendetta, which will result in mounting debts, more misery and a misplaced hatred that could damage your health as well as your bank balance.

SAVING £100s

www.adslogans.co.uk
www.skype.co.uk

www.thisismoney.co.uk/get-out-of-debt

The art of eco-driving

Heavy people pay more to drive, that's the conclusion (well sort of) of the motoring organisation the AA, which has devised a list of money-saving tips that, they say, can reduce your fuel consumption by between 10 and 15%.

If you fill up with £50 of petrol a week, these tips could save nearly £400 without using your car any less than you need to. Here's what they say you should consider:

REGULAR SERVICING Get the car serviced regularly.

ENGINE OIL Make sure you use the correct specification of engine oil.

TYRE PRESSURE Check tyre pressures regularly and before long journeys. Under-inflated tyres create more resistance and use more fuel.

LOSE WEIGHT Extra weight means extra fuel, lose the excess baggage from the boot.

STREAMLINE Roof racks/boxes create extra wind resistance and so increase fuel. Remove or pack carefully to reduce the drag.

DON'T GET LOST Plan unfamiliar journeys. Check the traffic news before you go.

COMBINE SHORT TRIPS Cold starts are inefficient so it pays to combine errands such as dropping-off the recycling or collecting the kids.

LEAVE PROMPTLY Don't start the engine until you're ready to go. This avoids fuel wastage while the car idles and ensures the engine warms up as quickly as possible.

REMOVING ICE Scrape ice rather than leave the car idling for a long period to warm up.

EASY DOES IT Drive smoothly, accelerate gently and read the road ahead to avoid unnecessary braking.

DECELERATE SMOOTHLY When you have to slow down or to stop, decelerate smoothly by releasing the accelerator in time, leaving the car in gear.

ROLLING If you can keep the car moving all the time, so much the better. Stopping then starting again uses more fuel than keeping rolling.

CHANGE UP EARLIER Change gear as soon as possible without laboring the engine – try changing up at an engine speed of around 2000rpm in a diesel car or around 2500rpm in a petrol car – it can make a big difference to fuel consumption.

CUT DOWN ON THE AIR-CON It increases fuel consumption at low speeds, but at higher speeds the effects are less noticeable. So if it's a hot day it's more economical to open the windows around town and save the air conditioning for high-speed driving.

TURN IT OFF Any electrical load increases fuel consumption, so turn off your heated rear windscreen, blowers and headlights when you don't need them.

STICK TO THE LIMITS Drive at or within the speed limit – the faster you go the greater the fuel consumption – and pollution. Driving at 70mph uses up to 9% more fuel than at 60mph and up to 15% more than at 50mph – 80mph can use up to 25% more fuel than at 70mph.

DON'T BE IDLE If you do get caught in a queue, avoid wasting fuel by turning the engine off if it looks like you could be waiting for more than three minutes.

USE YOUR HEAD Don't drive too close to the car in front if you value your brake pads and don't take the gas guzzler to drop the kids of at the school around the corner.

SAVING £100s

www.theaa.com

www.thisismoney.co.uk/better-driving

97 Don't lose the plot – if you can get one, that is

A few years ago allotment sites were under used and under threat as beady-eyed property developers circled with a view to turning these havens of municipal arable land over to houses or, more, likely "luxury" flats. (Luxury, *n. colloq.* Not very well built.)

Fast forward to now and the individual plots are becoming more difficult to get hold of than a dentist who'll provide NHS treatment or a banker who'll say sorry. Waiting lists are over a decade in some parts.

It is nevertheless always worth putting your name down because the idea of an allotment is much more romantic than getting out there in the rain and digging and weeding and digging some more and many people lose interest after the first season. If you are lucky enough to get one, consider a half-plot to start with. Half will be plenty big enough to cope with unless you are retired and have all the time there is for full-on amateur farming.

Once you've cleared and prepared the soil you're on your way. From then on, you'll have to dedicate at least an hour a week; that really is the absolute ground zero of least-ness, it is going to take up a lot more time that you think and if you miss a week, you have to make up time with time added because the weeds don't stop growing because you failed to show up.

It is inevitable that you will meet plot-holders who have been doing it for years and have all sorts of advice and produce to share, particularly spinach for some reason, but this is your canvas and you can try anything. Growing your own food is creating life itself and if you put in the effort you will be amazed what comes up, matures and ripens if and when the sun comes out.

If you're dedicated you can often get two crops a year and you really can feed a family during the warmer months and into autumn with your produce. If you've got a local Wilkinson store or similar you can find packets of seeds for pence and if you can start seeds off in a tray on a windowsill – even better.

The only things you need to worry about are your back – don't overdo it or you may never properly recover – the ethical dilemma of how you are going to deal with slugs and snails, and the task of washing the crops once you've harvested them. For this is real food, grown naturally, and though it will taste like nothing you buy at the supermarket, it's caked to high heaven in soil and may have any number of bugs on a shared tenancy in between every single leaf. Maybe that's why property developers value the land so much. After all, our lives are merely a pale if slightly fancy imitation of nature, and all.

If you can't get a plot or aren't prepared to put in the work, at least consider composting. You can find out everything you need to know and buy hugely subsidised compost bins at *Recycle Now*. Just make sure you've got the space – some of those bins are rather large.

SAVING £100s, but you've got to work for it

www.thisismoney.co.uk/the-plot

vegboxrecipes.co.uk

www.wilkinsonplus.com

www.recklessgardener.co.uk

www.gardenersworld.com

www.recyclenow.com

98 Tips in brief

Here are a few more quick tips that are pretty self-explanatory and well worth considering in your quest to cut back while still enjoying yourself.

BUY GENERIC MEDICINES Own-brand ibuprofen, aspirin, and cold remedies can cost 10 times less than the Nurofens, Night Nurses and Lemsips of this pharmaceutical world. How bad is that headache now?

CONSIDER A GENERIC MP3 PLAYER for £20 rather than an iPod, which can cost £100+

BEWARE THE FALSE BARGAIN Sometimes it's worth paying a bit more for quality.

SEND GIFT VOUCHERS FOR CHRISTMAS PRESENTS so that when the sales start in earnest the recipients can get double the value.

IF YOU USE AN A NATIONAL-RATE 0870 NUMBER to phone a company to sort out a problem of their making, ask them to call you back. Otherwise check out www.saynotoo870.com for lists of the regular phone numbers behind the money-making ones.

IF YOU'RE DRINKING WINE IN A BAR share a bottle of wine rather than buying by the glass.

USE AN INDEPENDENT GARAGE to service your car rather than a dealership.

SCARE YOURSELF INTO SAVING by working out how much you'll have to live on in retirement – and how much you need to save at *www.pensioncalculator. org.uk, www.thisismoney.co.uk/pension-calculator*

REMEMBER a con man (or woman) will be your friend, offer something for nothing, explain that you will save money, that you must do what you're told and do it now, will spin a tale to win your sympathy, twist the truth and take your money.

IF IT'S TOO GOOD TO BE TRUE IT USUALLY IS.

MAKE AN ICEBERG for your children to play with in the bath – just freeze water in an ice cream container.

CHECK OUT HYPNOTIST AND LIFESTYLE ADVISER *www.paulmckenna.com* for tips on killing cravings, change habits and losing weight – you could save a fortune.

THE LATEST MARKETING WHEEZE If you have time to spend hours trawling for special offers then check out the plethora of voucher sites such as *www.vouchercodes.co.uk*. They're a form of marketing designed to get you to buy more of what you don't want. Sometimes you can get lucky but usually you'll get 50p off your weekly shop.

SAVING £100

www.thisismoney.co.uk/money-savers

99 What First Direct did – a stark warning

Image this if you would.

Every three days you pay your bank £1 – but only if you *can't* afford it. It sounds so implausible that it can only have been dreamt up by either a bank or, no ... it *was* a bank – and that bank was First Direct. Since 2006, any First Direct customer who earns less than £25,000 a year must pay £120 a year, or £1 every three days, to maintain their bank account.

While there is a set of silly get-out clauses to avoid this fee such as taking products you probably don't want, pensioners, nurses, teachers and women on maternity leave are clearly seen as an unnecessary irritation. The marketing department dresses up the charge thus: "Banking with First Direct usually costs £10 a month, but it's free when you pay in at least £1,500 to your 1st Account each month, or hold a selected first direct additional product, or maintain an average monthly 1st Account balance of £1,500."

With hindsight, it is perhaps not such a bad idea. After all, it was irresponsible banking involving America's poorest people that created the credit crunch. So you could argue that restricting access to banking for people on low-income is a good move. For the bank.

If you do bank with First Direct and suddenly your income drops or you lose your job, watch out – you may be liable to pay their "poor tax".

SAVING £120 plus any subsequent overdraft charges

www.thisismoney.co.uk/first-direct-squirming
www.thisismoney.co.uk/find-a-new-bank-account

" The large print giveth and the small print taketh away. "

HOW TO SURVIVE THE CREDIT CRUNCH

100

READ THE SMALL PRINT

If you want to play the National Lottery online you have to click the box to say you have read and understood the terms and conditions – or "small print". The thing is, that for the National Lottery the terms and conditions are more than 37,000 words long. That's more words than this book! (Make your own jokes up about reading and understanding this book later, in your own time, please.) Some of Shakespeare's plays aren't much longer than 37,000 words. And he was really good. But you wouldn't want to read a whole one before you could log on to play a game.

That's small print for you. Satan's get-out clause and a burial ground for bad news. Luckily, when banks tweak their small print, they're obliged to tell you. Luckier still, there are clever people at *This is Money*, *Financial Mail* and *Money Mail* who have seen it all before and who have met many of the leading figures in the financial world who are responsible for much of the misery we're now facing. Our journalists will read the small print for you and if there are any catches snuck in by mistake, which there often are, they'll pick up on it and let you know either on the website or in our newspapers. The companies won't like it and the PRs will be on the phone to try to kill the story, usually starting with some revolting positive spin they've concocted before turning to anger and their lawyers.

We still have a free Press in the UK and if you keep reading and believing we can get through this mess together. Don't ever rely on journalists to give you all the information you need. What are you? Stupid? By all means read what we have to say and try to read between the lines because often – as in the case of the now bankrupt buy-to-let investment companies and the Icelandic banks – we cannot legally say what you would like us to. If you check back in our archives, you'll find that the warning signs were all there, published within the limits of our libel laws. And often the signs are there buried in the small print the companies hope no-one will read.

www.thisismoney.co.uk/newsletter
www.thisismoney.co.uk/the-iceland-pr-man

101

HELP!

"You asked me once, what was in Room 101. I told you that you knew the answer already. Everyone knows it. The thing that is in Room 101 is the worst thing in the world." George Orwell. *1984*.

Welcome to the last tip in the book: 101 – the number of the room where your own nightmares can happen.

Or at least that's how George Orwell saw it in *1984*, his classic tale of a dystopian world of surveillance and Government ownership. Sound familiar, anyone?

But this is not a tip at all. What? Didn't you read Tip 100!!!? Wow, we've still got a long way to go but I've run out of pages. It just leaves me space to say thank you for buying, borrowing or accepting this book. All the links within were chosen in good faith, not because they earn money for me from the highest bidder, but because I thought they'd be either useful, interesting or entertaining in our quest to get through the next few years with our sanity intact and our bank balances in a slightly better shape.

If you want to know more, or indeed you know better, I have created a special message board on *This is Money* for anyone who has enjoyed this book (and the other people who didn't), to discuss the issues and make suggestions. This is just the start.

Cheers, and good luck.

Richard Browning

SAVING Go to bed now. It will be better in the morning. If not let's talk about.

www.thisismoney.co.uk/101

The End.

A BIT ABOUT THE AUTHOR AND HOW THE BOOK CAME ABOUT

Richard Browning has been a journalist on and off for more than 20 years...

I've worked as a reporter, sub editor and theatre critic for local and national newspapers, including the *Daily Mail*, for trade and consumer magazines and the Press Association newswire. I spent nearly two years writing comedy sketches for radio and TV and one year as a ship's agent in France. Since the beginning of the millennium I've worked for *This is Money*, where in 2004, I began work on a piece called "50 ways to save money".

At the time, as far as I could see, nothing like it had been published and I felt it was time to share my experiences. I mentioned earlier that by 1999 debt had become an unmanageable burden for many people, well, by 2004 it was getting seriously out of control.

My hope was that having survived the last recession with big debts – although small by today's standards – indebted readers might start to sort their finances if given a light-hearted nudge in the right direction.

"50 ways" took a long time to compile but was worth every moment. It is one of the most popular articles on the site and I know people enjoyed it and that it made a difference because I've had emails from around the world saying so. The piece has been imitated many times – usually by the lazy and feckless – and talked about on various radio shows. Parts of it have been lent to newspapers, magazines and websites – and stolen by several others.

And now, thanks to Studio Cactus, it has grown into a book.

AUTHOR ACKNOWLEDGEMENTS

This book would not be possible without the team that conceived and kicked off *This is Money* in its first year: editor Wayne Asher, designer and developer Marty Gardner, designer Steve Dawson, writer Alison Potter and development editor Bridie Pritchard. Or its next generation of editors Guy Dresser, Alan Hill, Steve McDowell and Simon Moon and writers David Budworth, Michael Clarke, Sascha Hutchinson, Helen Loveless, Jamie Milne, Helen Monks and Jo Thornhill.

This is Money would not have developed one of the most intelligent and helpful message-board communities were it not for Dave Killeen and Ilana Fox, the dedication and knowledge of hosts, KK and Muriel, or the hundreds of regular contributors who share their advice and views every day to strangers across the country – and the world.

The site would be nothing without the incredibly talented team of journalists that currently create the content and keep the site updated seven days a week. Gillian Bevis, Tara Evans, Simon Lambert, Adrian Lowery, Ed Monk, Sylvia Morris, Alan O'Sullivan, Andrew Oxlade, Philip Scott. It really would be nothing were it not for design and technical geniuses James Hicking and Matt Gleeson. The book would be nothing without the efforts of the team at Studio Cactus and our product manager Nicole Cummings. And none of the tips in the book would have written had they not been tried and tested by some truly wonderful people, including Isabelle, Emilie, Pauline, Mike, Chris, Leisl, Huguette and Yves.

Finally, a special word of thanks to Salvatore, a sterling friend who helps tend my allotment when back trouble sometimes prevents any more than a few minutes digging – potential plot-holders, you have been warned. And to Bridie for proof reading the manuscript and making suggestions that turned the book into a "must read" rather than a mere "nice to have".

Thank you.

PUBLISHER'S ACKNOWLEDGEMENTS

Studio Cactus would like to thank Richard Browning and the magnificent team at *This is Money* for all their hard work and for their truly fabulous website. Special thanks to Nicole Cummings and Andrew Oxlade for helping to get the project off the ground. Thanks also to Hugh Brune of Portfolio for his faith in the project and for his infectious enthusiasm. Thanks to Jennifer Close for her editorial expertise and Sharon Cluett for her wonderful styling and Jacket design. Thanks to Kevin Jones and Laurence of kja-artists.com for the cover illustration. Special thanks also to Beth Stevens for proof reading the book and for her work in the very early stages of this project, especially for her magnanimity in recognising that Richard Browning had already produced a list of saving tips that couldn't be bettered: "the original and the best". Finally, special thanks to Claire Moore, Clive Goddard and Harriet Sanders.